LANCASI

A GENEALOGICAL BIBLIOGRAPHY

Volume 3

Lancashire Family Histories and Pedigrees

by

Stuart A. Raymond

Published by the
Federation of Family History Societies (Publications) Ltd.,
The Benson Room, Birmingham & Midlands Institute,
Margaret Street, Birmingham, B3 3BS, U.K.

Copies also obtainable from:

S.A. & M.J.Raymond, 6, Russet Avenue, Exeter, EX1 3QB, U.K.

First published 1996

Cataloguing in publication data:

Raymond, Stuart A., 1945- . *Lancashire: a genealogical bibliography.* 3 vols. British genealogical bibliographies. Birmingham: Federation of Family History Societies, 1995. v.3. Lancashire family histories and pedigrees.

DDC: 016.9291094276

ISBN: 1-86006-023-4

ISSN: 1033-2065

Printed and bound by Oxuniprint, Walton Street, Oxford OX2 6DP

Contents

Introduction

This bibliography is intended primarily for genealogists. It is, however, hoped that it will also prove useful to historians, librarians, archivists, research students, and anyone else interested in the history of Lancashire. It is intended to be used in conjunction with my *English genealogy: an introductory bibliography,* and the other volumes in the *British genealogical bibliographies* series. A full list of these volumes appears on the back cover.

Published sources of information on Lancashire genealogy are listed in volumes 2 and 3 of the present work; this volume lists works devoted to specific families, together with collections of pedigrees, biographical dictionaries, genealogical directories, and works on heraldry and surnames. It includes published books and journal articles, but excludes the innumerable notes and queries to be found in family history society journals, except where the content is of importance. Where I have included such notes, replies to them are cited in the form 'see also', with no reference to the names of respondents. I have also excluded extracts from newspapers, and histories which have not been published. Where possible, citations are accompanied by notes indicating the period covered, the locality/ies in which the families concerned dwelt, and other pertinent information.

This volume partially supersedes:
HORROCKS, SIDNEY, ed. *Lancashire: family histories, pedigrees, heraldry.* A contribution towards a Lancashire bibliography 4. Manchester: Joint Committee on the Lancashire Bibliography, 1972.

Horrocks did, however, give locations for all the works he identified, and this information may still be useful (although it may now be out of date). Unlike the present work, Horrocks included typescript and manuscript works, and should be consulted to identify these.

Be warned: just because information has been published, it does not necessarily follow that it is accurate. I have not made any judgement on the accuracy of most works listed: that is up to you.

Anyone who tries to compile a totally comprehensive bibliography of Lancashire is likely to fall short of his aim. The task is almost impossible, especially if the endeavour is made by one person. That does not, however, mean that the attempt should not be made. Usefulness, rather than comprehensiveness, has been my prime aim — and this book would not be useful to anyone if its publication were to be prevented by a vain attempt to ensure total comprehensiveness. I am well aware that there are likely to be omissions, especially in view of the fact that, given constraints of time and money, it has not been possible for me to visit all of the large number of libraries with substantial collections on Lancashire's history. Each of them may well possess works not held anywhere else. The identification of such works is not, however, a major aim of this bibliography. Rather, my purpose has been to enable you to identify works which are mostly readily available, and which can be borrowed via the inter-library loan network irrespective of whether you live in London or Melbourne. Most public libraries are able to tap into this network; your local library should be able to borrow most items I have listed, even if it has to go overseas to obtain them.

If you are an assiduous researcher, you may well come across items I have missed. If you do, please let me know, so that they can be included in the next edition.

The work of compiling this bibliography has depended heavily on the resources of the libraries I have used. These included Lancashire County Library's Local Studies Department at Preston, the Harris Library, also at Preston, Lancashire Record Office, Manchester Public Library, Exeter University Library, Exeter City Library, the British Library, and the Society of Genealogists, amongst others. I am grateful to the librarians of all these institutions for their help. Brian Christmas and Rita Hirst both kindly read and commented on early drafts of the book, Jean Smith typed the manuscript, and Bob Boyd saw the book through the press. I am grateful too to the officers of the Federation of Family History Societies, whose support is vital for the continuation of this series. My thanks also to my wife Marjorie, and to Paul and Mary, who have lived with this book for many months.

Stuart A. Raymond

Abbreviations

B.D.F.H.S.	Bolton and District Family History Society
C.F.H.S.N.	*Cumbria Family History Society newsletter*
C.S.	Chetham Society
C.W.A.A.S.Tr.	Cumberland & Westmorland Antiquarian & Archaeological Society transactions
F.H.S.	Family history society
H.S.L.C.	*Historical Society of Lancashire and Cheshire proceedings/transactions*
L.	*Lancashire [Journal of the L.F.H.H.S.]*
L.C.A.N.	*Lancashire and Cheshire antiquarian notes.*
L.C.A.S.	Transactions of the Lancashire and Cheshire Antiquarian Society
L.C.R.S.	Lancashire and Cheshire Record Society
L.F.H.	*Liverpool family historian*
L.F.H.H.S.	Lancashire Family History and Heraldry Society
L.F.H.S.J.	*Liverpool Family History Society journal*
L.P.R.S.	Lancashire Parish Register Society
M.G.	*Manchester genealogist*
M.G.H.	*Miscellanea genealogica et heraldica*
M.L.F.H.S.	Manchester & Lancashire Family History Society
N.W.C.H.	*North West catholic history*
N.S.	New series
O.S.	Old series
P.N.	*Palatine notebook*
R.S.G.H.[L]	Rossendale Society for Genealogy and Heraldry [Lancashire] N.B. This was the original name of the L.F.H.H.S.

Bibliographic Presentation

Authors' names are in SMALL CAPITALS. Book and journal titles are in *italics*. Articles appearing in journals, and material such as parish register transcripts, forming only part of books are in inverted commas and textface type. Volume numbers are in **bold** and the individual number of the journal may be shown in parentheses. These are normally followed by the place of publication (except where this is London, which is omitted), the name of the publisher and the date of publication. In the case of articles, further figures indicate page numbers.

Libraries and Record Offices

There are many libraries and record offices holding collections relating to Lancashire genealogy; they cannot all be listed here. For a full listing, see:

WYKE, TERRY, & RUDYARD, NIGEL, eds. *Directory of local studies in North West England* Bibliography of North West England 14. Manchester: Bibliography ..., 1993.

Amongst the most important collections are:

Local Studies Dept.,
Lancashire County Library,
143, Corporation Street,
PRESTON,
Lancashire, PR1 2UQ

Lancashire Record Office,
Bow Lane,
Preston,
Lancashire, PR1 2RE

Record Office and Local History Dept.,
Liverpool Libraries and Information Services,
Central Library,
William Brown Street,
Liverpool, L3 8EW.

Manchester and Lancashire Family History Society,
Clayton House,
59, Piccadilly,
Manchester.

Local Studies Unit,
Manchester Central Library,
St. Peter's Square,
Manchester, M2 5PD.

1. GENEALOGICAL DIRECTORIES

A great deal of work on the history of Lancashire families is currently in progress. A number of national directories of genealogists' interests are available; these are listed in *English genealogy: a bibliography*. A number of directories of Lancashire researchers are also available; these include:

British Isles genealogical register, 1994: Lancashire Section. 4 fiche. Birmingham: Federation of Family History Societies, 1994. Frequently referred to as the *Big R*.

LANCASHIRE FAMILY HISTORY & HERALDRY SOCIETY. *Members' interest list*. 2 fiche. [ ]: L.F.H.H.S., 1995.

HOWARD, KEN. *Directory of members interests 1991*. 1 fiche. Liverpool: Liverpool & S. W. Lancashire F.H.S., 1991.

MANCHESTER & LANCASHIRE FAMILY HISTORY SOCIETY. *Members interest directory*. Manchester: M.L.F.H.S., 1994. Regular supplements in *M.G.*

ORMSKIRK & DISTRICT FAMILY HISTORY SOCIETY. 'Members interests as at 30th September 1994', *O.D.F.H.* **8**, 1994, i-xxviii.

2. SURNAMES

The origins of surnames have implications for genealogists. The authoritative study is:

MCKINLEY, RICHARD. *The surnames of Lancashire*. English surnames series **4**. Leopard's Head Press, 1981.

Other studies include:

FISHWICK, LT. COL. 'The distribution of surnames in Lancashire in the sixteenth and seventeenth centuries', *H.S.L.C.* **53**, N.S., **17**, 1901, 131-8. Brief.

LEECH, E. BOSDIN. 'Surnames in Lancashire', *L.C.A.S.* **58**, 1945-6, 177-204. General discussion.

MARCH, H.C. *East Lancashire nomenclature & Rochdale names*. Simpkin & Co., 1880. Includes discussion of Rochdale surnames.

'The surnames in early Manchester Independent registers', *M.G.* **20**(4), 1984, 103-4. For 1770-99.

HUNT, THOMAS. 'A note on some Heywood surnames', *Transactions of the Rochdale Literary and Scientific Society* **4**, 1983-5, 649.

FISHWICK, HENRY. 'Rochdale surnames', *Transactions of the Rochdale Literary and Philosophical Society* **3**, 1891-2, 31-51.

3. BIOGRAPHICAL DICTIONARIES

A number of works provide brief biographical information on leading Lancastrians. The series of 'contemporary biographies' published at the turn of the century by W.T. Pike is particularly noteworthy:

PIKE, W.T., ed. *A dictionary of Edwardian biography: Lancashire.* Edinburgh: Peter Bell, 1986. Facsimile reprint of the 'contemporary biographies' portion of *Lancashire at the opening of the twentieth century: contemporary biographies.* originally published Brighton: W. T. Pike, 1903.

PIKE, W. T., ed. *A dictionary of Edwardian biography: Manchester & Salford.* Edinburgh: Peter Bell, 1987. Facsimile reprint of the biographical portion of *Manchester and Salford at the close of the 19th century: contemporary biographies.* Originally published Brighton: W. T. Pike, 1899.

PIKE, WILLIAM THOMAS, ed. *A dictionary of Edwardian biography: Liverpool.* Edinburgh: Peter Bell, 1987. Facsimile reprint of the biographical portion of *Liverpool and Birkenhead in the twentieth century: contemporary biographies,* originally published Brighton: W. T. Pike, 1911.

See also:

DREDGE, JOHN INGLE. 'Notable persons connected with Lancashire and Cheshire', *P.N.* **2**, 1882, 195-6. List of entries in Thompson Cooper's *New biographical dictionary* 1873.

ESPINASSE, FRANCIS. *Lancashire worthies.* Simpkin Marshall & Co., 1874. 2nd series, 1877. Chapter length biographies.

ORCHARD, B. GUINNESS. *Liverpool: legion of honour.* Birkenhead: the author, 1893. Primarily a biographical dictionary.

READ, GORDON. *Lancashire history makers.* Wakefield: E.P. Publishing, 1975. 12 brief biographies of famous Lancastrians.

'Bolton obituaries', *M.G.* **27**(2), 1991, 40-41. From *Old South-East Lancashire: a genealogical magazine,* published in 1880.

4. COLLECTIONS OF FAMILY HISTORIES AND PEDIGREES

A number of studies on the 'county' families of Lancashire are available. These include:

CROSTON, JAMES. *The county families of Lancashire and Cheshire.* Manchester: John Heywood, 1887. Includes chapters on the families of Stanley, Egerton, Trafford, Warburton, Harrington, Grey, Molyneaux, Hulton, Grosvenor, Mosley, Mainwaring, Hesketh and Davenport.

FOSTER, JOSEPH. *Pedigrees of the county families of England, vol. 1: Lancashire.* Head, Hole and Co., 1873.

LOFTHOUSE, JESSICA. *Lancashire's old families.* Robert Hole, 1972. Studies of over 40 'county' families.

ORMEROD, GEORGE. *Miscellanea Palatina: consisting of genealogical essays illustrative of Cheshire and Lancashire familes, and of a memoir of the Cheshire Domesday roll.* T. Richards, 1851. Includes notes, pedigrees, etc., relating to the families of Norres, Aldford, Arderne, Banastre, Bredbury, Done, Fitzroger, Gernet, Lathom, Montalt, Orreby, Stanley and Stokeport. Mainly medieval.

ORMEROD, GEORGE. *Parentalia: genealogical memoirs.* [ ]: Thomas Richards, 1851. Genealogical notes on the families of Ormerod, Johnson, Wareing, Crompton, Nuthall, Norres, Latham, Lathom, Arderne, and De Montalt.

RYLANDS, J. PAUL. 'Some Lancashire pedigrees drawn about the years 1425-1440', *M.G.H.* 5th series, **1**, 1916, 247-52 & 281-5. Beamont, Pilkington, Southworth, Radcliffe, Hoghton, Harington, Legh, Halsall and Bradshaw families.

5. HERALDRY

A. *Visitation Pedigrees*

In the sixteenth and seventeenth centuries, the heralds undertook periodic 'visitations' of the counties in order to determine the right of gentry to bear arms. In so doing, they compiled large collections of pedigrees. For a brief introduction to this material, see:

FISHWICK, H. 'The Heralds', *L.C.A.S.* 2, 1884, 39-45.

An index to the manuscript pedigrees has been published, although this is now largely superfluous in view of the more recent publication of the pedigrees listed:

ORMEROD, GEORGE. 'Calendars of the names of families which entered their several pedigrees in the successive heraldic visitations of the County Palatine of Lancaster', in *Chetham miscellanies* 1. C.S., O.S., 24, 1851. Separately paginated.

For a collection of letters concerning the right of the Heralds to conduct visitations, see:

RAINES, F.R., ed. 'Letters on the claims of the College of Arms in Lancashire, in the time of James the First, by Leonard Smethley and Randle Holme, deputy heralds', *Chetham miscellanies* 5. C.S., O.S., 96, 1875. Separately paginated.

For the actual pedigrees, see:

LANGTON, WILLIAM, ed. *The visitation of Lancashire and a part of Cheshire, made in the twenty-fourth year of the reign of King Henry the Eighth, A.D. 1533, by special commission of Thomas Benalt, Clarencieux.* C.S., O.S., 98 & 110. 1876-82.

RAINES, F.R., ed. *The visitation of the County Palatine of Lancaster, made in the year 1567, by William Flower, esq., Norroy King of Arms.* C.S., O.S., 81. 1870.

RAINES, F.R., ed. *The visitation of the County Palatine of Lancaster made in the year 1613, by Richard St. George, esq., Norroy King of Arms.* C.S., O.S., 82. 1871.

RAINES, F.R., ed. *The visitation of the County Palatine of Lancaster, made in the year 1664-5, by Sir William Dugdale, Knight, Norroy King of Arms.* C.S., O.S., 84-5 & 88. 1872-3.

Two related works are:

RYLANDS, J. PAUL. 'Disclaimers at the Heralds' visitations', *H.S.L.C.* 43-4; N.S., 7-8, 1891-2, 63-90. Mainly in Cheshire, 1613-64, also Lancashire, 1667.

'A fragment of Sir Wm. Dugdale's visitation of Lancashire from a manuscript in the possession of F.R.Raines', in *Chetham miscellanies* 1. C.S., O.S., 24, 1851, separately paginated. List of persons in Salford Hundred not answering the Heralds' summons, 1665.

B. *Funeral certificates*

The heralds were also responsible for organising the funerals of armorial gentry. This involved drawing up funeral certificates which, *inter alia*, list all the mourners present. Lancashire funeral certificates have been published in:

KING, THOMAS WILLIAM, ed. *Lancashire funeral certificates.* C.S., O.S., 75. 1869. Covers 1568-1675.

RYLANDS, J. PAUL, ed. *Cheshire and Lancashire funeral certificates, A.D., 1600 to 1678.* L.C.R.S. 6. 1882.

See also:

BANKES, JOYCE H.M. 'The funeral of Meyrick Bankes of Winstanley, 1827', *H.S.L.C.* 112, 1960, 159-66. Includes hatchment.

'Funeral certificates', *M.G.H.* 1, 1868, 85-8. Relating to the Aston, Norres and Glascor families of Lancashire and Cheshire.

'Funeral certificates: Cheshire, Lancashire, Shropshire and North Wales', *M.G.H.* 1, 1868, 27-35. Relating to the Massey, Dore, Bunbury, Holford, Brerwood, Brereton, Green, Bretterghe, Cholmondeleigh, Poole, Legh, Leech, Bestone and Sutton families.

'Funeral certificates', *M.G.H.* 1, 1868, 43-6. Relating to the Fletcher, Leigh, Broughton, Martyn *alias* Dukenfield, Allen and Gerrard families of Cheshire and Lancashire, 1598-1601.

In a way, newspaper reports of funerals are the modern equivalent of funeral certificates. Two such reports have recently been reprinted:

SAGAR, JOHN. 'Councillor William Campy's obituary', *L.* 4(4), 1983, 8-10. From the *Accrington gazette,* 1899, giving names of many mourners from the Clayton le Moors area.

'An Accrington obituary: George Whitaker (1903)', *L.* **6**(1), 1985. 29. Lists mourners.

C. General heraldry

Here are listed a number of general works on Lancashire heraldry. Quite a number of brief notes on heraldic subjects are also found in *L*. Many of these, however, are not of specifically Lancashire interest.

BOUMPHREY, R.S., HUDLESTON, C.ROY, & HUGHES, J., eds. *An Armorial for Westmorland and Lonsdale*. Cumberland & Westmorland Antiquarian & Archaeology Society, Extra series, **21**. 1975. See also **23**. 1978.

FRANCE, R. SHARPE. 'An index of Lancashire heraldry', *H.S.L.C.* **92**, 1940, 101-32.

RYLANDS, JOHN PAUL. 'Two Lancashire rolls of arms *temp* Edward III and Henry VIII', *H.S.L.C.* **37**; N.S., **1**, 1885, 149-60.

RYLANDS, W. H. 'Some Lancashire and Cheshire heraldic documents', *H.S.L.C.* **63**; N.S., **27**, 1912, 178-219. Heraldic notes on many families.

RYLANDS, J. PAUL. 'A manuscript containing Lancashire church notes and trickings of arms, made in the years 1564 to 1598', *H.S.L.C.* **42**; N.S., **6**, 1890, 255-74. Heraldic notes.

D. Family Heraldry

Aspinwall

See Blackburne

Banastre

'The arms of Banastre and of Langton', *Herald and genealogist* **8**, 1874, 440-46. Medieval.

Blackburne

RYLANDS, J. PAUL. 'Grant of the arms of Green and Aspinwall as quarterings to John Blackburne, esq., 11th May, 1803', *Genealogist* N.S., **34**, 1918, 87-8.

Blundell

G., T.E. 'The arms of Blundell, of Ince-Blundell, Lancashire', *P.N.* **1**, 1881, 57-8. See also 108-10 & 129.

'Arms of Blundell', *M.G.H.* **1**, 1868, 66. 17th c.

Brockholes

LARAWAY, EDWARD. 'Heraldry for genealogist and armorist', *L.* **13**(3), 1992, 17-19. Brockholes family heraldry.

Butler

RYLANDS, J. PAUL. 'Patents of arms to the Butlers of Bewsey and Kirkland', *H.S.L.C.* **67**; N.S., **31**, 1915, 148-58. 16th c.

'Arms of Blundell', *M.G.H.* **1**, 1868, 66. 17th c.

Clare

'Grant of arms to William Clare of Walton on the Hill in the County of Lancaster, gentleman, 1846', *M.G.H.* 5th series **2**, 1916-17, 122.

Clayton

BAILEY, REGINALD THRELFALL. 'Sculptured Clayton arms at Otterspool, formerly in Water Street, Liverpool', *H.S.L.C.* **75**; N.S., **39**, 1923, 178-85. Also includes notes on Tarleton family, 18th c.

Clifton

LARAWAY, EDWARD. 'Heraldry for genealogist and armorist', *L.* **12**(4), 1991, 35-7. Clifton family heraldry.

Del Bothe

RYLANDS, J. PAUL. 'Private grant of arms from Thomas de Barton to John Del Bothe, of Barton, Co. Lanc., A.D.1403', *L.G.* **1**, 1879-80, 19-27.

Dugdale

'Grant of arms to Adam Dugdale of Dovecote House, Liverpool, 1833', *M.G.H.* 3rd series **2**, 1898, 7.

'Grant of crest to John Dugdale of Clitheroe, 2 Eliz.', *M.G.H.* N.S., **4**, 1884, 103.

Faryngton

CROOKS, FREDERIC. 'Armorial seal of William de Faryngton', *H.S.L.C.* **83**, 1931, 97-100. Includes pedigree, 13-15th c.

'Confirmation of arms, and alteration of crest, to William Ffaryngton, of Worden, Co. Lancaster, by Lawrence Dalton, Norroy, 16 December 1560', *M.G.H.* **1**, 1868, 61-2.

Gardener
'Grant of arms to Robert Gardener of Lancashire, 2 Edward VI', *M.G.H.* 3rd series **3**, 1900, 141.

Gerard
LARAWAY, EDWARD. 'Heraldry for genealogist and armorist', *L.* **13**(2), 1992, 27-9. Gerard family heraldry.

Golightly
MISTLETOE. 'Armorial bookplate of Richard Golightly', *M.G.H.* 4th series **3**, 1910, 1. 18-19th c.

Green
See Blackburne

Haighton
TOPPING, J.M. 'The arms of Haighton of Chaigley', *L.* **7**(2), 1986, 27.

Hesketh
LARAWAY, EDWARD. 'Heraldry for genealogist and armorist', *L.* **13**(4), 1992, 27-9. Hesketh family, 13-20th c.

Heyworth
'Grant of arms to Lawrence Heyworth of Yewtree, in the parish of West Derby, Co. Lancaster, esq., M.P., and to the descendants of his father, Peter Heyworth, gentleman, A.D. 1856', *Genealogist* **7**, 1883, 88-9.

Hoghton
'Grant of crest to Richard Hoghton of Park Hall, Co. Lancaster, 1606', *M.G.H.* 3rd series **1**, 1896, 193.

Langton
See Banastre

Legh
'An ancient augmentation', *Genealogical magazine* **1**, 1897-8, 17-21. Legh of Bradley, 1665.
'Grants of arms', *Genealogist* **5**, 1881, 142-6. Includes grant to Legh of Newton in Makerfield, 1806.

Leyland
'Grants of arms', *Genealogist* **5**, 1881, 184-5. Includes grant to John Leyland of Hindley, 1863.

More
'Grants and confirmations of arms and crests', *M.G.H.* 5th series **10**, 1938, 10-12. Includes grant to More of Kirkdale, 1561.

Pearson
'Grant and confirmation of arms, by Garter, Clarenceaux and Norroy, to Henry Robert Pearson of London, gentleman, sometime chief clerk in Her Majesty's Treasury, and to the other descendants of his later father, John Pearson of London ... and also to the descendants of his late uncle Thomas Pearson of Manchester, gentleman, A.D. 1865', *Genealogist* **7**, 1883, 231-2.

Radclyffe
LARAWAY, EDWARD. 'Heraldry for genealogist and armorist', *L.* **13**(1), 1992, 23-5. Radclyffe family heraldry.

Ridgway
RYLANDS, J. PAUL. 'Examples of armorial bookplates: Ridgway', *M.G.H.* N.S., **3**, 1880, 47. Of Cheshire and Lancashire; includes genealogical notes, 19th c.

Royds
'Grant of arms by Sir Isaac Heard, Garter, to James Royds of Mount Falinge, Co. Lancaster, 1820', *M.G.H.* 2nd series **3**, 1890, 293-4.

Sanderson
See Stubbs

Schofield
'Grant of a crest to Cuthbert Schofield esq. of Schofield Hall, Rochdale, in 1583', *L.G.* **1**(12), 1880, 472-6.

Smallshaw
RYLANDS, J. PAUL. 'Grant of arms to Dorothy Smallshaw [of Bolton] spinster, 1750', *L.G.* **1**(9), 1880, 355-7.
See also Stubbs

Stanley
BAILEY, F.A. 'Some Stanley heraldic glass from Worden Hall, Lancashire', *H.S.L.C.* **101**, 1949, 69-84.

LARAWAY, EDWARD. 'Heraldry for genealogist and armorist', *L.* **14**(1), 1993, 27-8. Stanley family, Earls of Derby.

Townley
T., F.J. 'The book-plate of Charles Townley, esq., York Herald', *Journal of the Ex Libris Society* **10**, 1900, 26-7. 18th c.

Stubbs
'Grant of arms', *Genealogist* **4**, 1880, 286-90. Includes grants to Joseph Stubbs of Warrington, 1849, Dorothy Smallshaw of Bolton le Moors, 1750, and Richard Withington Bromley Sanderson of Cheetham, 1869.

Whittle
CROOKS, FREDERIC. 'Armorial seal of Alexander de Whittle', *H.S.L.C.* **80**, 1929, 52-3. 14th c.

Willoughby
WILLOUGHBY, HIGSON PHILIP. 'The heraldry of the Lancashire Willoughbys', *Coat of arms* **9**, 1966-7, 283-92. 17-18th c.

6. DIARIES, JOURNALS ETC.

Diaries and journals frequently contain much information of use to genealogists. For instance, the diary of William Fisher, listed below, notes many births, marriages and deaths. Many Lancashire diaries have been published; the following list is selective. Ten studies of Lancashire diarists are included in:
BAGLEY, JOHN JOSEPH. *Lancashire diarists: three centuries of Lancashire lives.* Phillimore, 1975.

Angier
HEYWOOD, OLIVER. *Oliver Heywood's life of John Angier of Denton, together with Angier's diary, and extracts from his 'An helpe to better hearts'; also Samuel Angier's diary.* C.S., N.S., **97**, 1937. Includes John Angier's will, 1677.

Assheton
RAINES, F.R., ed. *The journal of Nicholas Assheton of Downham, in the County of Lancaster, esq. for part of the year 1617, and part of the year following, interspersed with notes from the life of his contemporary John Bruen of Bruen Stapleford in the County of Chester, esq.* C.S., O.S., **14**. 1848. Includes brief genealogical notes on Assheton, with pedigree shewing relationship to Greenacres and Lister. Mentions many names of contemporaries.

Blundell
BLUNDELL, NICHOLAS. *Blundell's diary and letter book, 1702-1728,* ed. Margaret Blundell. Liverpool: Liverpool University Press, 1952. Many names. Includes pedigree of Blundell of Crosby, 12-20th c.
BLUNDELL, NICHOLAS. *The great diurnal of Nicholas Blundell of Little Crosby, Lancashire,* transcribed by Frank Tyrer; ed. J.J. Bagley. 3 vols. *L.R.C.S.* **110, 112, & 114**. 1968-72. Covers 1702-28. Includes pedigrees, 17-18th c., including those of the related families of Butler of Ireland and Langdale of Holne.

'Lancashire mortuary letters, 1666-1672, from the Crosby letters'. *H.S.L.C.* **36**, 1884, 33-52. Letters from William Blundell, noting many deaths.

Brockbank
TRAPPES-LOMAX, RICHARD, ed. *The diary and letter book of the Rev. Thomas Brockbank, 1671-1709.* C.S., N.S., **89**. 1930. Includes pedigrees of Brockbank, of Turnley, Whittingham and Chippendale, of Leyburn and Witham, and of Toulson. Mentions many names.

Byrom
BYROM, JOHN, ed. *The private journal and literary remains of John Byrom,* ed. Richard Parkinson. C.S., O.S., **32, 34, 40, & 44.** 1854-7. 1707-63. Includes folded pedigrees of the Byrom families of Byrom, Salford, and Manchester, 14-19th c.

Fisher
ROLLINSON, WILLIAM, & HARRISON, BRETT, eds. *The diary of William Fisher of Barrow, 1811-1859.* Occasional paper, **16.** Lancaster: Centre for North-West Regional Studies, 1986. Entries largely concerned with births, marriages and deaths.

Halstead
HOLGATE, ELIZABETH. 'The diary of John Halstead of Knave Hill, Great Marsden', *L.* **5**(4), 1984, 15-17. Extracts of obituaries, *etc.,* early 19th c.

Heywood
HEYWOOD, OLIVER. *The Rev. Oliver Heywood, B.A., 1630-1702: his autobiography, diaries, anecdote and event books, illustrating the general family history of Yorkshire and Lancashire ...* ed. J.Horsfall Turner. 4 vols. Brighouse: A.B. Bayes, et al, 1881-5.

Hodgkinson
WOOD, FLORENCE, & WOOD, KENNETH, eds. *A Lancashire gentleman: the letters and journals of Richard Hodgkinson, 1763-1847.* Stroud: Alan Sutton, 1992.

Hulton
HOGG, ANTHONY. *The Hulton diaries, 1832-1928: a gradely Lancashire chronicle.* Chichester: Solo Mio, 1989. Includes pedigrees, 18-20th c.

Jackson
CASSON, T.E. 'The diary of Edward Jackson, vicar of Colton, for the year 1775', *C.W.A.A.S.Tr.* N.S., **40,** 1940, 1-45. Many local names.

Kay
BROCKBANK, W., & KENWORTHY, F., eds. *The diary of Richard Kay, 1716-51, of Baldingstone, near Bury, a Lancashire doctor.* C.S., 3rd series, **16.** 1968. Many names.

Martindale
MARTINDALE, ADAM. *The life of Adam Martindale written by himself,* ed. Richard Parkinson. C.S., O.S., **4.** 1845. 17th c.

Newcome
HEYWOOD, THOMAS, ed. *The diary of the Rev. Henry Newcome from September 30, 1666 to September 29, 1663.* C.S., O.S., **18.** 1849. Of Manchester.
NEWCOMBE, HENRY. *The autobiography of Henry Newcome, M.A.,* ed. Richard Parkinson, C.S., O.S., **26-7.** 1852.

Reynolds
GREG, EMILY, ed. *Reynolds-Rathbone diaries and letters, 1753-1839.* [Edinburgh]: T. & A. Constable, 1905. Includes pedigrees of Reynolds and Rathbone, 18-19th c.

Satterthwaite
SCHOFIELD, M. M. 'The letter book of Benjamin Satterthwaite of Lancaster, 1737-1744', *H.S.L.C.* **113**, 1961, 125-67. Includes pedigree, 17-18th c.

Stout
STOUT, WILLIAM. *The autobiography of William Stout of Lancaster, 1665-1752,* ed. J. D. Marshall. C.S., 3rd series, **14.** 1967. Includes folded pedigree, 17-19th c.

Tyldesley

TYLDESLEY, THOMAS. *The Tyldesley diary: personal records of Thomas Tyldesley (grandson of Sir Thomas Tyldesley the royalist) 1712-1713-1714*, ed. Joseph Gillow & Anthony Hewitson. Preston: A. Hewitson, 1873. Many names.

Watkin

WATKIN, ABSALOM. *Diaries of Absalom Watkin: a Manchester man, 1787-1861*, ed. Magdalen Goffin. Stroud: Alan Sutton, 1993.

7. FAMILY HISTORIES

Abram

'Abram family of Abram, County Lancaster', *Local notes and gleanings from the Manchester Guardian* **106**, 1876, 2-3. See also **108**, 1976, 2-3. 15-17th c.

Adams

AXON, GEOFFREY R. 'Roger and Orion Adams, printers', *L.C.A.S.* **39**, 1921, 108-24. 18th c.

Adlington

ABRAM, W.A. 'Adlington family of Adlington, Co. Lancaster', *P.N.* **5**, 1885, 4-5. 14-17th c.

Ainscough

HARTLEY, MARY. 'The Ainscough family of Mawdesley, in the parish of Croston, Lancashire', *Catholic ancestor* 3(4), 1991, 136-8. Pedigree, 16-18th c.

Ainscow

See Cronshaw

Ainsworth

AXON, ERNEST. 'Harrison Ainsworth's paternal ancestors', *L.C.A.S.* **27**, 1909, 33-49. Includes pedigree of Ainsworth of Blacklow and Spotland.
See also Harrison and Langley

Allanson

'Allanson Bible', *M.G.* 22(4), 1986, 123-4. 18-19th c.

Almond

See Longworth

Almorice

See Liverpool

Ambrose

DUNSTON, F. 'Ambrose', *Pedigree register* **1**, 1907-10, 62-3. Of Ormskirk; pedigree, 16-18th c.
FISHWICK, LT. COL. 'The Ambrose family of Lowick and Woodplumpton, Co. Lancashire', *Local gleanings* **1**, 1879-80. 99-108.
See also Roscoe

Anderton
TEMPEST, ARTHUR CECIL, MRS. 'An episode in the Anderton family history', *H.S.L.C.* **42**; N.S., **6**, 1890, 181-94. 15-16th c. dispute; includes folded pedigree.

Antrobus
ANTROBUS, REGINALD L., SIR. *Antrobus pedigrees: the story of a Cheshire family.* Mitchell Hughes and Clarke, 1929. Also of Manchester; 15-20th c.

Arkwright
FITTON, R. S. *The Arkwrights: spinners of fortune.* Manchester: Manchester University Press, 1989. 16-19th c. *See also* Strutt

Armitage
ARMITAGE, CYRUS. *Some account of the family of the Armitages from 1662 to the present time.* Reed & Pardon, 1850.
I'ANSON, ARTHUR B. *The history of the Armytage or Armitage family.* Hazell Watson & Viney, [1915]. Also of Yorkshire, *etc.* Medieval-20th c.

Ashawe
'The Ashawes, Hultons, Bartons, Ashetons and Radcliffes', in BARTON, B.T., ed. *Historical gleanings of Bolton and District [third series].* Bolton: Daily Chronicle Office, 1883, 261-7. Medieval.

Ashburner
HELSBY, THOMAS. *Pedigree of the family of Ashburner, Co. Lancaster.* Taylor & Co., 1872. 17-19th c.
'Ashburner', *M.G.H.* N.S., **1**, 1874, 224-31. Of India; also of Dalton in Furness, Gleaston, Scales and Kensington; pedigree, 17-19th c.

Asheton
See Ashawe

Ashton
ASHTON, CHARLES. 'The Ashton family of Croston', *M.G.* **19**(4), 1983, 97-101. See also **19**(1), 1984, 39. 15-20th c.

VENN, J. 'Notes on the family of Ashton of Penketh, Co. Lancaster, with special reference to John Penketh, who was executed for his adherence to the Jacobite cause, 28th January 1691,' *H.S.L.C.* **38**; N.S., **2**, 1886, 1-14. Includes wills, parish register extracts, *etc.,* with pedigrees, 17th c.

Ashworth
ASHWORTH, ALF. 'A Lancashire family, 9: Ashworth of Rochdale & Bolton,' *L.* **7**(1), 1986, 17-21. Includes pedigree, 19-20th c.
ASHWORTH, ALF. 'The direct ancestry of Ashworth/Entwistle of Bolton, c.1800-1987,' *L.* **9**(2), 1988, 25-30. 19-20th c.
BOYSON, RHODES. *The Ashworth cotton enterprise: the rise and fall of a family firm, 1818-80.* Oxford: Clarendon Press, 1970. Includes Ashworth pedigree, 16-20th c.

Askew
BROWNBILL, J. 'The Askews of Marsh Grange,' *C.W.A.A.S.Tr.* N.S., **10**, 1910, 331-41. 16th c.

Asmunderlaw
SKELTON, JOSEPH. 'The De Asmunderlaws of Furness and Cumberland', *C.W.A.A.S.Tr.* N.S. **39**, 1939, 59-64. Includes folded pedigree, 12-15th c.

Aspden
HOWARTH, ARTHUR. 'A Lancashire family, 27: Aspden of Aspden, Burnley, and Cliveger', *L.* **11**(3), 1990, 25-33. Includes pedigree, 16-17th c.
HOWARTH, ARTHUR. 'Aspden/Astin of Habergham Eaves and Worsthorne, 2: back to the 17th century?', *L.* **10**(4), 1989, 34-6. Includes pedigree, 18th c.

Aspinall
REDMONDS, G. 'Lancashire surnames in Yorkshire: the distribution and development of Aspinall and Ridehalgh in the West Riding', *Genealogists' magazine* **18**(1), 1975, 13-18.
See also Aspinwall

Aspinwall
ASPINALL, HENRY OSWALD. *The Aspinwall and Aspinall families of Lancashire, A.D. 1189-1923: a collection of family records brought together.* Exeter: William Pollard & Co., 1923. Includes abstracts of wills, parish registers, *etc.,* with pedigrees, 14-20th c.
ASPINALL, H.O. 'The Aspinwall and Aspinall families of Lancashire', *Genealogist* N.S., **32-7**, 1916-21, *passim.* Incomplete; includes pedigrees, 13-19th c.

Assheton
BEATTY, JOSEPH M. 'Assheton of Salford, and Penn of Pennsylvania', *Notes and queries* 12th series **8**, 1921, 345-6. 17th c.
BEATTY, JOSEPH M. 'The descent of the Asshetons of Salford and Pennsylvania from the Asshetons of Shepley', *Notes and queries* **193**, 1948, 208-11. Includes pedigree, 17-18th c.

Astin
HOWARTH, ARTHUR. 'The Astin family of Worsthorne, 1: back to c.1800 (including connection with Crabtree of Bridestone and Pickles of Worsthorne)', *L.* **10**(2), 1989, 12-20. 18-19th c.
See also Aspden

Atherton
ATHERTON, RALPH S. 'Further beyond the Workhouse: Atherton of Alston and Preston', *L.* **11**(3), 1990, 38-41. 18-19th c.
BROWN, JOHN C. J. 'The Atherton family in England', *New England historical and genealogical register* **35**, 1881, 67-72. 17-18th c.
E., J.P. 'The Atherton family', *P.N.* **4**, 1884, 14-15. See also 34-5. 13-18th c.
HOPE, T.H. *Notes on the Athertons of Atherton.* Leigh: D.& J. Forbes, 1892. Medieval-18th c.

Audley
'Pedigree xx: Audley of Liverpool', in READE, ALEYN LYELL. *Audley pedigrees.* Percy Lund Humphries & Co., pt. 3, 1936, 257-313. 18-19th c.

Aughton
AUGHTON, PETER. 'The King of the cocklers', *L.F.H.* **7**(2), 1985, 30-33. Includes pedigree of Aughton of North Meols, 18-19th c.

Aynesargh
See Liverpool

Backhouse
FOSTER, JOSEPH. *The descendants of John Backhouse, yeoman, of Moss Side, near Yealand Redman, Lancashire.* 2 vols. Chiswick Press, 1894. 17-19th c., includes wills and pedigrees of many other families.

Bahr
BEHREND, ARTHUR. *Portrait of a family firm: Bahr, Behrend & Co., 1793-1945.* Liverpool: The author, 1970.

Baldwin
BARROW, GEOFFREY. 'An ecclesiastical record: the Baldwin family', *L.* **5**(1), 1984, 28-9. Of Leyland, 18-20th c.
See also Woodcock

Banastre
L., W. 'Notice of the family of Robert Banastre, one of the benefactors of Basingwerk Abbey', *Archaeologia Cambrensis* **1**, 1846, 334-46. Banastre family of Newton in Makerfield; medieval.

Bankes
G., E.B. 'Bankes of Bank Newton and Winstanley', *Notes and queries* **169**, 1935, 154. See also 264-5 & 302-4. 16-17th c.
See also Woodcock

Banks
STOTT, BRIAN. 'A Lancashire family, 24: Banks of Bridge End, Rimington', *L.* **10**(4), 1989, 23-8. Includes pedigree, 18-19th c.

Barbauld
RODGERS, BETSY. *Georgian chronicle: Mrs. Barbauld & her family.* Methuen & Co., 1958. Includes pedigree, 17-19th c.

Barcroft

RUNK, EMMA TEN BROECK. *Barcroft family records: an account of the family in England, and the descendants of Ambrose Barcroft the emigrant of Solebury, Pennsylvania.* Philadelphia: J.B. Lippincott, 1910. Includes pedigrees (some folded), 16-19th c.

'The Barcroft family of Lancashire', *P.N.* **4**, 1884, 135. 17th c.

Barlow

BARLOW, ANGELA. 'He thought he saw a buffalo ...', *M.G.* 24(3), 1988, 160-64. Barlow family; includes pedigree, 18-19th c.

'Barlow Hall, Lancashire and its lords', *P.N.* **4**, 1884, 205-14 & 229-35. Barlow family, 13-16th c., included pedigree.

'The index to the first series of the Camden Society: the Barlow family', *P.N.* **2**, 1882, 198-9. Entries concerning the Barlow family of Lancashire in a major record society series.

Barrow

FRANCE, R. SHARPE. 'Direct male ancestry of Sir John Barrow from 1602', *C.W.A.A.S.Tr.* N.S., **74**, 1974, 222-3. 17-18th c.
See also Paulet

Barton

BARTON, BERTRAM FRANCIS. *Some account of the family of Barton, drawn from manuscripts and records, together with pedigrees of the various branches of the house.* Dublin: Cahill & Co., 1902. 17-20th c., includes pedigrees.

DEAN, JOHN. 'The ancient lords of Middleton, part II: the Barton family', *L.C.A.S.* **16**, 1898, 102-33. Includes folded pedigree, 14-15th c.
See also Ashawe and Rigby

Bayley

AXON, ERNEST. *The family of Bayley of Manchester and Hope.* The author, 1894. Reprinted with additions from *L.C.A.S.* **7**, 1889, 193-28. 17-18th c.

Baynes

CHIPPINDALL, W.H. 'The Baynes family of Sellet Hall in Whittington', *C.W.A.A.S.Tr.*, N.S., **28**, 1928, 63-77. Includes folded pedigree, 14-17th c., and wills.

CHIPPINDALL, W.H. 'Robert Baynes of Littledale in Caton, Co. Lancaster, standard bearer to Sir Edward Stanley at Flodden Field, and his descendants', *C.W.A.A.S.Tr.*, N.S., **41**, 1941, 54-71. 15-19th c., includes pedigree.

Beakbane

BEAKBANE, RENAULT. *Beakbane of Lancaster: a study of a Quaker family.* Kidderminster: Ken Tomkinson, 1977. 16-20th c.

Behrend
See Bahr

Belfield

BELFIELD, HERBERT E. *The Belfield family.* Adlard & Son, 1930. Of Lancashire, Hertfordshire, Devon and the United States; includes folded pedigrees in pocket, 13-20th c.

EARWAKER, J.P. 'The Belfield family of Clegg near Rochdale', *L.C.A.N.* **1**, 1885, 41-5 & 50-53. Includes 16th c. schedule of 46 deeds dating back to 1311.

Benison

'The Benisons of Hornby', *P.N.* **3**, 1883, 261-2. 16-18th c.

Berewe
See Paulet

Berington
See Whittingham

Beswicke
See Royds

Bethell

'In search of James Bethell: an artist working from 1827-1835', *L.* **13**(4), 1992, 31-6. Includes pedigree, 18-19th c.

Bibby

BIBBY, JOHN P. *The Bibbys of Conder Mill and their descendants.* Liverpool: J. P. Bibby, 1979. 18-20th c., includes pedigree. *See also* Statham

Billinge

BILLINGS, F.H., & BILLINGS, M.A. *Billinge of Billinge: 1000 years of a Lancashire catholic family,* ed. A.M.Billings. St. Albans: Billing Family History, 1988. Includes pedigrees.

Bindloss

ROPER, WILLIAM OLIVER. 'Borwick Hall', *H.S.L.C.* 47; N.S., 9, 1895, 21-36. Bindloss family, 16-17th c.

Binns

SAXTON, EVELINE B. 'The Binns family of Liverpool and the Binns collection in the Liverpool Public Library', *H.S.L.C.* 111, 1959, 167-80. Includes pedigree, 18-19th c. The Binns collection forms the nucleus of Liverpool Record Office.

Birch

BIRCH, HERBERT. *Memories of Birch: its owners and its ancient chapel.* Manchester: [ ], 1896. Reprinted from the *Manchester City News.* Birch family, 14-18th c.

GOULDSON, JOAN EVALINE. *The Birch tree: a history of the Birch family of Sefton in general, and of Walter Edward Birch in particular.* Bovey Tracey: the author, 1992, 18-19th c.

'Birche of Birche', *M.G.H.* 1, 1868, 305-8. Pedigree, medieval-17th c., of Lancashire and Herefordshire. *See also* Bradburn

Birtwistle

ASPDEN, RAY. 'The Birtwistle family, 1210-1850', L. 11(2), 1990, 16-18.

ASPDEN, RAY. 'Birtwistle of Goodshaw, Rossendale: from manorial court rolls', *L.* 10(1), 1989, 20-24. Includes pedigree, 1470-1670.

BIRTWISTLE, WILLIAM A. *The Birtwistle family, 1200-1850 A.D.* Blackburn: W.A.Birtwistle, 1990. Includes many pedigrees and tables.

Bisley

'Bisley memoranda', *M.G.H.* N.S., 2, 1877, 276-7. Brief notes, 15-18th c.

Bispham

BISPHAM, WILLIAM. *Memoranda concerning the family of Bispham in Great Britain and the United States of America.* New York: Gilliss Brothers, 1890. Medieval-19th c., originally of Lancashire. Includes folded pedigree.

Blackburne

RYLANDS, J.P. *Hale Hall, with notes on the family of Ireland Blackburne.* Liverpool: privately printed, 1881. Ireland family, 14-18th c., Blackburne family, 18-19th c. Includes pedigrees.

Blundell

ANDERSON, D. 'Blundell's collieries: the progress of the business', *H.S.L.C.* 116, 1964, 69-116. Includes Blundell family pedigree, 17-18th c.

GIBSON, T.E. 'A century of recusancy illustrated from the records of the Blundells of Crosby', *H.S.L.C.* 31; 3rd series, 7, 1879, 33-66. 16-17th c.

TYRER, FRANK. 'The recusant Blundells of Crosby', *N.W.C.H.*, 1972-3, 27-51. 16th c.

Boddington

'Boddington pedigree', *M.G.H.* N.S., 2, 1877, 244-7. Of Shropshire and Lancashire, *etc.,* pedigree, 18-19th c.

Bold

See Statham

Bolton

BOLTON, HENRY CARRINGTON, & BOLTON, REGINALD PELHAM. *The family of Bolton in England and America, 1100-1894: a study in genealogy.* New York: Privately printed, 1895. Reprinted Calgary: P.C.Bolton, 1989. Includes folded pedigree, 17-20th c. Originally of Blackburn.

BOLTON, ROBERT. *Genealogical and biographical account of the family of Bolton in England and America, deduced from an early period, and continued down to the present time ....* New York: John A. Gray, 1862. Originally of Blackburn; also of Yorkshire and the United States. Includes folded pedigree, 12-19th c.

Bond
DRACOS, ELIZABETH. 'A Lancashire family, 14: Bond of Preston and Lancaster', *L.* **27**(8), 1987, 18-25. Includes pedigree, 17-20th c.

Booker
BOWKER, CHARLES E.B. 'Notes as to the family of Booker or Bowker: extracts from the parish registers of Prestwich church, Lancashire, 1603-1750', *M.G.H.* N.S., **4**, 1884, 316-7.
BOWKER, CHARLES E.B. 'Notes as to family of Bowker or Bouker: registers of Blackley Chapel, Manchester', *M.G.H.* 2nd series, **3**, 1890, 124-5. 17-18th c., includes monumental inscriptions.
See also Bowker.

Booth
JOHN, A.H. *A Liverpool merchant house: the history of Alfred Booth and Company, 1863-1958.* George Allen & Unwin, 1959. Includes pedigree of Booth, 18-20th c.
AXON, ERNEST. 'The family of Bothe (Booth) in the 15th and 16th centuries', *L.C.A.S.* **53**, 1938, 32-82. Of Barton upon Irwell.
BOOTH, WILLIAM HENRY. 'The Booths of Bury', *Bury and Rossendale historical review* **2**, 1910-11, *passim*. Medieval-19th c.
TALLENT-BATEMAN, CHAS.T. 'The family of Humphrey Booth, founder of Salford chapel', *L.C.A.S.* **27**, 1909, 115-44. 16-17th c.
TYNDALE, O.M. 'The Booths in Warrington during the Civil War', *L.C.A.S.* **64**, 1954, 55-65.
WRIGHT, ANNIE. 'Booths of Redivals', *L.* **4**(2), 1983, 8-9. 16-19th c.
'Booth of Orford, in the parish of Warrington, Co. Lancaster', *M.G.H.* 3rd series **3**, 1900, 7. Written notes from printed book, 18th c.
See also Spencer

Borron
'Borron of Warrington', *M.G.H.* N.S., **1**, 1874, 354-5. Pedigree, 17-19th c.

Bostock
BOSTOCK, A.J. 'History of the Bostock family', *Lancashire and Cheshire historian* **1**, 1965, 221-2 & 245-6; **2**, 1966, 301-4; **3**, 1967, 577-80. Medieval; includes pedigree.

Bothe
See Booth

Bowker
MITFORD-BARBERTON, IVAN, & MITFORD-BARBERTON, RAYMOND. *The Bowkers of Tharfield.* Oxford: University Press, 1952. Tharfield is in South Africa. The family originated in Lancashire; also of Gateshead, Co. Durham. 16-20th c.
See also Booker

Bradburn
VIGEON, EVELYN V. 'The celebrated cookie shop: a history of the Eccles cake shops and their owners, with a note on the Bradburn family of Eccles', *M.G.* **29**(1), 1993, 33-50. Includes pedigrees of Birch, 18-19th c., and Bradburn, 18-19th c.

Braddyll
CURWEN, JOHN F. 'Pedigree comprehending the descents of the families of Braddyll of Brockholes, Dodding of Dodding Green, and Gale of Whitehaven ...', *C.W.A.A.S.Tr.* N.S., **8**, 1908, 382(f). Folded pedigrees, 16-19th c. Dodding Green, Westmorland; Whitehaven, Cumberland.

Bradshaigh
HAWKES, ARTHUR JOHN. *Sir Roger Bradshaigh of Haigh, Knight and Baronet, 1628-1684, with notes of his immediate forebears.* Manchester: Lancashire and Cheshire Antiquarian Society, 1945. Supplement to *L.C.A.S.* Also published in *Cm.S.* N.S., **109**, 1945. Includes folded pedigree, 12-20th c., shewing links with Norris and Lindsay; also will of Roger Bradshaigh, 1641.
AXON, ERNEST. 'A note on the Bradshaigh roll', *L.C.A.S.* **25**, 1907, 159-67. Bradshaw family of Haigh.
EDWIN-COLE, JAS. 'The heiress of Bradshaigh of Haigh', *Herald and genealogist* **8**, 1874, 186-7. 18th c.

STANNING, J.H. 'Bradshaigh or Bradshaw, Co. Lanc.' *L.C.A.N.* **1**, 1885, 68-9. Includes medieval pedigree.

Bradshaw
'The Bradshaw of Bradshaw &c', in BARTON, B.D., ed. *Historical gleanings of Bolton and District [third series]*. Bolton: Daily Chronicle Office, 1883, 254-61. Medieval. *See also* Bradshaigh and Urm(e)ston

Braithwaite
BRAITHWAITE, G.E. *The Braithwaite clan.* Ledbury: L.Tilley & Son, [197-?] Medieval-19th c.

BRAITHWAITE, G.E. *Braithwaites of Hawkshead, Ambleside, Burnside and Kendal, 1332-1964.* Kendal: Wilson, [1965?]

Bretherton
See Stapleton

Brettargh
FORMBY, CUTHBERT. 'The Brettarghs of Ince Blundell', *H.S.L.C.* **86**, 1934, 93-106. 17-19th c.

FRANCE, R. SHARPE. 'The poor Brettarghs of Penketh', *H.S.L.C.* **99**, 1947, 89-93. 17th c.

STEWART-BROWN, R. 'The Brettarghs of Brettargh Holt in Woolton', *H.S.L.C.* **88**, 1937, 211-39. Includes pedigree, 14-20th c.

Bridge
BARNES, JANICE. 'A Lancashire family, 25: the Bridges of Hawkshaw Lane', *L.* **11**(1), 1990, 22-7. Pedigree, 18-20th c.

Briercliffe
BRIERCLIFFE, R.D., BRIERCLIFFE, T.H., & AXON, ERNEST. 'The Briercliffes of Briercliffe', *L.C.A.S.* **35**, 1917, 50-91. Includes pedigree, 12-19th c.

Bromley
HAWKES, A.J. *The Bromley family of Wigan in the 18th century.* [Wigan]: [Wigan Observer], 1939. Reprinted from the *Wigan Observer.*

Brook
See Ferguson

Brooke
HARWOOD, H.W. FORSYTH. 'The true descent of Brooke of Astley', *Genealogist* N.S., **13**, 1897, 222-8. 17-18th c., includes wills.

LOCKETT, R.C. 'Richard Brooke of Handford *vel* Handforth and Liverpool, F.S.A; some notes concerning his lineage and connections', *H.S.L.C.* **62**; N.S., **26**, 1910, 175-81. 17-18th c.

Brown
TALLENT-BATEMAN, C.T. 'Manchester street lore, XII: Brown Street', *[Manchester] City news notes and queries* **7**, 1887-8, 285-6. See also **8**, 1889-90, 43-4.

Brownlow
ANDERTON, H.INCE 'The Brownlow family of Hall i' th' Wood', *H.S.L.C.* **63**; N.S., **27**, 1912, 66-77. Includes eight deeds relating to Tonge, 17th c., with pedigree, 15-17th c.,

Bucknall
See Mellard

Butterworth
ANGUS-BUTTERWORTH, L.M. 'Notes on the family of Butterworth of Belfield', *Transactions of the Rochdale Literary and Scientific Society* **19**, 1935-7, 107-27. Medieval-19th c.

FISHWICK, HENRY. 'Notes on the Butterworths of Belfield', *Transactions of the Rochdale Literary and Scientific Society* **7**, 1900-3, 26-9. 16-18th c.

Byrom
ABRAM, W.A. 'The Byrom family of Byrom, parish of Winwick', *L.C.A.N.* **2**, 1886, 91-100. See also 153-5. 17-18th c.

See also Byron

Byron
BYRON, MARK BENNETT. *The Byron chronicle: a history of the Byron and Byrom families, 1066-1800.* Derby, Connecticut: the author, 1965. Of Lancashire and Virginia, *etc.*

Calverley
See Royds

Carruthers
CARRUTHERS, A.STANLEY., & REID, R.C. *Records of the Carruthers family.* Elliot Stock, 1934. Includes many pedigrees, including that of Carruthers of Barrow in Furness, 19-20th c.

Carter
WRIGHT, W. BALL. 'Carter of Yorkshire, Manchester and Ireland', *Pedigree register* 2, 1910-13, 204-11. Pedigree, 16-19th c.

Cartmel
'The Cartmel family bible', *M.G.* 12(3), 1976, 77-8. 17-19th c.

Carus
CARUS-WILSON, HERBERT, & TALBOYS, HAROLD J., eds. *Genealogical memoirs of the Carus-Wilson family, being an account (1320-1899) of the families of Carus of Kendal; Carus of Halton, Co. Lancs., Carus of Melling and Kirkby Lonsdale; Wilson and Carus-Wilson of Casterton, Co. Westmorland and Carus-Wilson of Penmount, Co. Cornwall.* Hove: Emery and Son, 1899. Medieval-19th c.

Chaderton
'Chaderton pedigree', *M.G.H.* 1, 1868, 160. 17th c.

Chadwick
CHADWICK, EDMUND & BOARDMAN, JAMES. *Report on the estate of Sir Andrew Chadwick and the proceeding of the Chadwick Association in reference thereto ... to which is prefixed 'the life and history of Sir Andrew Chadwick, being a record of investigations as to his extraction, parenting and immediate relations and particulars of his estate, by John Oldfield Chadwick.* Simpkin Marshall & Co., 1881. Includes folded pedigree, 18-19th c.

COOKSON, BARBARA. 'Nil desperandum', *Catholic ancestor* 4(2), 1992, 58-62. Includes Chadwick family pedigree, 18-20th c.

HIRST, RITA. 'The Chadwick Association, 2: the search for a rightful heir', *L.* 12(1) 1991, 32-43. Includes pedigree, 17-19th c.

Charles
'The Charles family chronology', *M.G.* 12(1), 1975, 9-13. 1762-1878.

Charnock
ABRAM, W.A. 'Ancient Lancashire families, III: the Charnocks of Leyland Old Hall', *L.C.A.N.* 2, 1886, 3-11. 15-18th c.

Chetham
RAINES, FRANCIS & SUTTON, CHARLES, W. *Life of Humphrey Chetham, founder of the Chetham Hospital and Library, Manchester.* C.S., N.S., 49-50. 1903. Includes 'Chetham genealogies: pedigrees of the families of Chetham of Cheetham, Nuthurst, Middleton, Crumpsall, Smedley and Castleton in Lancashire, and of Great Livermere in Suffolk', by Ernest Axon, as an extensive appendix. Also includes will of Humphry Chetham, 1653/4, with list of feoffees and masters of Chetham Hospital, 1651-1902, and librarians of Chetham Library, 1651-1883.

Chorley
WILSON, JOHN. *The Chorleys of Chorley Hall: extracts from the Chorley parish registers, &c., and an attempt at a family history.* Manchester: Sherratt and Hughes, 1907. Medieval-19th c.

Chorlton
'Origins of family names: the name of Chorlton', *M.G.* N.S., 27(1), 1965, 11-14.

Clarke
'Bible entries: Clarke and Lumb of Garstang', *M.G.H.* 4th series, 3, 1910, 319-30. 18-19th c.

Clayton
AVELING, THOMAS W. *Memorials of the Clayton family ...* Jackson, Walford and Hodder, 1867. 18th c.

GARDNER, JOAN M. 'A Lancashire family: Clayton of Preston', *L.* 9(4), 1988, 22-9. Includes pedigree, 18-19th c.

STEWART-BROWN, RONALD. 'The Tower of Liverpool with some notes on the Clayton family of Crooke, Fulwood, Adlington and Liverpool', *H.S.L.C.* 61; N.S., 25, 1909, 41-82. 17-18th c.

'The pedigree of the Claytons of Crooke, Fulwood and Adlington, in the County of Lancaster', *Genealogist* N.S., **26**, 1910, 129-42. 16-19th c.
See also Every-Clayton

Clegg
AINSWORTH, RICHARD. *The Clegg family of Huncoat.* [ ], 1929. Reprinted from the *Accrington observer and times.*
See also Royds.

Clifton
ABRAM, W.A. 'An old private birth and death register: Cliftons of Goosnargh and other families', *L.C.A.N.* **2**, 1886, 35-7. 18-19th c.
KENNEDY, JOHN. *The Clifton chronicle.* Preston: Carnegie Publishing 1990. Of Lytham, 18-20th c.

Clitherow
GANDY, MICHAEL J. 'The family of St. Michael Clitherow', *Catholic ancestor* 3(2), 1990, 50-54. Includes Clitherow pedigree, 16-17th c.

Cockerill
WOODCOCK, THOMAS. *William Cockerill and his family.* Haslingden: [Haslingden Observer?], 1927. 18-19th c.

Coddington
See Croslegh

Cook
See Walker

Cookson
COOKSON, MICHAEL D. 'Cooksons and the vanished hamlet of Cross Slack', *L.* 15(2), 1994, 25-32. Includes pedigree, 18-20th c.

Coop
TODD, ANDREW. 'A Lancashire family, 22: Coop of Booth: fire, feud and fatality at a Tottington farm', *L.* **10**(2), 1989, 20-31. See also **10**(4), 1989, 17-20. Includes pedigree, 18-20th c.

Cooper
LAITHWAITE, GILBERT, SIR. *Miscellaneous genealogical notes on the families of Cooper, Craik, Laithwaite, Lowe, Mathias, Pendlebury and Pilkington.* 3rd ed. Lahore: privately printed, 1968. 18-19th c.

Cornthwaite
SMITH, J.P. *Bishop Cornthwaite, his ancestors and relations.* [ ], 1924. Includes pedigree, 17-19th c.

Cort
HEWITT, C. 'The Cort family of Bolton, Chorley & Manchester', *M.G.* **18**(1), 1982, 16-17. Pedigree, 18-19th c.

Cowell
PRIESTLEY, KAY. 'Ann Hemming's husband: Cowell or Hornby of Fleetwood', *L.* **10**(3), 1989, 13-15. 19th c., of Bispham.

Cowlishaw
GREGSON, RUTH. 'Calling the Cowlishaw/Wilkinson family', *Family History Society of Cheshire journal* 21(2), 1991, 19-23. Entries in a family bible, 1680-1836; probably relates to Lancashire families.

Cowper
COWPER, H.S. 'The Cowpers of Aldingham', *C.W.A.A.S.Tr.* N.S., **21**, 1921, 81-95. Includes pedigree, 16-17th c., with will of Leonard Cowper, 1593.
See also Swainson

Crabtree
See Astin

Cragg
FANDREY, GEORGIANA. *The Craggs of Greenbank.* Saskatoon: Modern Press, 1977. 17-20th c., latterly of Canada.

Craig
See Cooper

Cranke
GAYTHORPE, HARPER. 'The Crankes of Urswick', *Barrow Naturalists Field Club and Literary and Scientific Association proceedings &c.* **18**, 1907, 103-6. 17-18th c.

GAYTHORPE, HARPER. 'Two old masters: the Crankes of Urswick', *C.W.A.A.S.Tr.* **6,** 1906, 128-42. 18th c.

'A young ladies school in Manchester in 1771', *Manchester notes & queries* **8,** 1891, *passim.* Primarily concerns the Cresswell family.

Croft

CARLISLE, NICHOLAS. *Notices of the ancient family of Croft, of the counties of Lancaster and York.* Shakespeare Press, 1841. Medieval-19th c.

Crofts

See Cronshaw

Crompton

BALLARD, ELSIE. *A chronicle of Crompton, together with a history of the families of Crompton and Milne, and of A. A. Crompton & Co., by J. E. Hargreaves.* Crompton: Crompton Urban District Council, 1967.

Cronshaw

DENHAM, C.H. *Some notes on the Cronshaws of Lancashire and allied families: Ainscow, Lang, Crofts, Meakin, Fergusson, Nuttall, Ford-Smith, Pope, Hawkins, Rogers, Holloway, Watkinson,* ed. Edward Phelps. Dublin: University Press, 1934. Includes folded pedigree, 17-20th c.

Crook

CROOK, SHEILA. 'Crooks of Tockholes and Bolton', *M.G.* **23**(3), 1987, 214-6. 19th c.

CROOKS, FREDERIC. *History of the Crooks family of Prescot, Huyton and St. Helens.* [Huyton]: privately published, 1924. 1220th c.

Crookes

CROOKE, ARTHUR CARLETON. *The Crookes of Pendle.* Ross on Wye: Planographic, 1980. 16-20th c., includes pedigree.

Cropper

CONYBEARE, F.A. *Dingle Bank: the home of the Croppers.* Cambridge: W. Heffer and Sons, 1925. 18-19th c., includes pedigree.

WATERHOUSE, N. *Memorials of the families of Cropper, Cubham, and Wolsey of Bickerstaffe, and of Winstanley of Winstanley.* Liverpool: D. Marples, 1864. 17-18th c.

Crosfield

CROSFIELD, JOHN FOTHERGILL. *The Crosfield family: a history of the descendants of Thomas Crosfeld of Kirkby Lonsdale, who died in 1614.* Rev. ed. Cambridge: University Press, 1980. Also of Lancashire.

Croslegh/Crossle/Crossley

CROSLEGH, CHARLES. *Descent & alliances of Croslegh or Crossle, or Crossley, of Scaitcliffe, and Coddington of Oldbridge; and Evans of Eyton Hall.* De La Mare Press, 1904. Includes pedigrees of many related families.

Cross

C[ROSS, RICHARD ASSHETON]. *A family history.* Eccle Riggs: [Privately published], 1900. Cross family; includes folded pedigree, 18-19th c.

Crosse

STEWART-BROWN, R. 'The Crosse family of Wigan, Chorley and Liverpool', *H.S.L.C.* **73**; N.S., **37,** 1921, 153-86. 14-18th c.

Crossley

'The late Mr. James Crossley', *P.N.,* **3,** 1883, 221-8. Includes pedigree of Crossley, of Lancashire and Yorkshire, *etc.,* 17-19th c.

Cubham

See Cropper

Culcheth

RYLANDS, J. PAUL. 'Culcheth of Cucheth, Co. Lancaster', *M.G.H.* N.S., **2,** 1877, 209-13. 13-18th c.

RYLANDS, J. PAUL. *Genealogies of the families of Culcheth of Culcheth, and Risley of Risley, both in the County of Lancaster.* Privately printed, 1876. Pedigrees, 13-18th c.

Cunliffe

OWEN, C.H. *The descendants of the elder branch of the Cunliffes of Wycoller.* 2nd ed. William Clowes & Sons, 1887. Mainly 18-19th c.

'Cunliffe pedigree', *M.G.H.* **2**, 1876, 22. 16-17th c.

'Document relating to the last members of the family of Cunliffe, of Wycoller Hall, near Colne', *L.C.A.N.* **2**, 1886, 105-12. 18th c.

See also Sparling

Dalton

ROPER, WILLIAM OLIVER. 'The Daltons of Thurnham', *H.S.L.C.* **42**; N.S., **6**, 1890, 97-124. Includes pedigree, 15-19th c., also will abstracts *etc.*

Daltry

ABEL, ROBERT L. 'Found on a fly leaf', *L.* 3(7), 1981, 12. Notes on the Daltry family of Oldham, early 19th c.

Dania

DANIA, VIVIAN. 'A Lancashire family: the Danias of Rochdale', *L.* 6(1), 1985, 18-21. Includes pedigree, 19-20th c.

Danvers

MACNAMARA, F.N. *Memorials of the Danvers family (of Dauntsey and Culworth), their ancestors and descendants, from the Conquest to the termination of the eighteenth century ...* Hardy & Page, 1895. Of Dauntsey, Wiltshire, Culworth, Northamptonshire, and various other places, including Liverpool. Includes pedigrees.

Darbishire

See Kay

Davies

'Extracts from the family bible of William & Hannah Davies (nee Stinchcombe)', *M.G.* 18(3), 1982, 78-9. 19th c.

See also Spencer

Dawes

See Willoughby

De Bardesey

CURWEN, JOHN F. 'Some notes on the De Bardesey family of Bardsey Hall, Furness', *C.W.A.A.S.Tr.* N.S., **6**, 1906, 175-83. Includes medieval pedigree.

De La Warre

See Grelley

Deacon

OWEN, J. 'The Deacons and the Waltons', *Manchester notes and queries* **7**, 1888, 82-3. 18th c.

See also Gamon

Dearden

DEARDEN, GORDON. 'A Lancashire family, 13: Dearden of Wolfenden and Holcombe', *L.* 8(1), 1987, 24-8. 15-17th c., with pedigree, 17-20th c.

TODD, ANDREW. 'Dubious Dearden ancestry at St. Chad's, Rochdale', *L.* 9(3), 1988, 42-6. See also 9(4), 1988, 18-21. Medieval.

Del Crosse

See Liverpool

Dent

WILLAN, T.S. *An eighteenth century shopkeeper: Abraham Dent of Kirkby Stephen.* Manchester: Manchester University Press, 1970. Includes pedigrees of Dent and Waller, 17-18th c.

Devis

PAVIERE, SYDNEY H. *The Devis family of painters.* Leigh on Sea: F.Lewis, 1950. 18-19th c., includes pedigree.

Diggle

MCALPINE, IAN. 'The Diggle family of Prestwich', *M.G.* 23(1), 1987, 20-21. 18th c.

'The Diggles of Booth Hall', *M.G.* 26(2), 1990, 54. Pedigree, 17-19th c.

Dinwiddie

MARLOW, A.V. 'The Dinwiddie and Grant families', *M.G.* 20(4), 1984, 105-8. Of Manchester, 18-19th c.

Dixon

DIXON, VANESSA. 'Dixon extracts from the parish church of St. Helens, Merseyside', *M.G.* 19(3), 1983, 70. Late 19th c.

Dodding

See Braddyll

Doodson

'The Doodson saga', *M.G.* 12(2), 1976, 46-8. 17-19th c.

Drinkwater
DRINKWATER, C.H., & FLETCHER, W.G.D. *The family of Drinkwater of Cheshire, Lancashire, and the Isle of Man, etc.* Fleet: E. Dwelly, 1920. Includes pedigree, 17-19th c., with many extracts from wills, parish registers, and monumental inscriptions, *etc.*

Dukinfield
RYLANDS, J. PAUL. 'A vellum pedigree of the families of Dukinfield, Co. Chester, and Holland of Denton, Co. Lancaster, drawn in the year 1622', *Genealogist* N.S., **32**, 1916, 85-90. 13-17th c.

Dunstan
COOK, N. P. 'John Dunstan and his family (1798-1874)', *Cheshire history* **21**, 1988, 34-6.

Dunster
MORIARTY, G. ANDREWS. 'Genealogical research in England: Dunster', *New England historical and genealogical register* **80**, 1926, 86-95. 16-17th c., includes wills etc.
'Dunster, Willard and Hills', *New England historical and genealogical register* **61**, 1907, 186-9. 16-17th c., of Bury.

Duxbury
ASPDEN, RAY. 'Duxbury of Upper Darwen: an outline guide to sources', *L.* **11**(3), 1990, 41-3. 17-18th c.

Earle
EARLE, T. ALGERNON. 'Earle of Allerton Tower', *H.S.L.C.* **42**; N.S., **6**, 1892, 15-76. Includes pedigrees, 16-19th c., extracts from parish registers, *etc.* Also of Frodsham, Cheshire.

Eccles
SMITH, J.P. 'Notes of the Eccles family of Meanfields, Lancashire', *Publications of the Catholic Record Society* **9**, 1911, 174-8. Includes pedigree, 18-19th c.

Eccleston
GIBLIN, J.F. 'The Eccleston family of Eccleston', *N.W.C.H.* **16**, 1989, 1-6. Medieval-18th c.

Egerton
'Egerton of Shaw', *M.G.H.* N.S., **2**, 1876, 16. Pedigree, 16-18th c.

Eland
CLAY, C.T. 'The family of Eland', *Yorkshire archaeological journal* **27**(107), 1924, 225-48. Medieval; includes pedigree.

Eltonhead
RANKIN, R.G. 'The Eltonhead family', *H.S.L.C.* **108**, 1955, 35-62. Medieval-17th c., includes pedigree.
See also Thompson

Emmott
HINDLE, H. 'Emmott Hall and the Emmotts', *L.* **12**(4), 1991, 18-20. 18-20th c.

Entwisle
GRIMSHAW, BANNISTER. *The Entwisle family.* Accrington: Accrington Gazette, 1924. Medieval-19th c.

Entwistle
See Ashworth

Essex
See Swainson

Evans
'Evans family of Eccles', *M.G.* **17**(1), 1981, 17. Pedigree, 18-19th c.
See also Croslegh

Every-Clayton
WHITTAKER, GLADYS. 'The Every-Claytons of Carr Hall', *L.* **5**(3), 1984, 12-15. 18-19th c.

Fairclough
FAIRCLOUGH, P.S. 'The Fairclough family of Aspull, Haigh and Wigan, Lancashire', *Catholic ancestor* **3**(5), 1991, 189-91. 18th c.
See also Townsend

Faithwaite
FAITHWAITE, J. R., & HINDE, THOMAS WINDER. *Faithwaite of Littledale, in Caton, County Lancaster.* Kendal: Titus Wilson & Son, 1924. Includes folded pedigree, 16-19th c.

Fallon

HIGSON, ANN. *The Fallons: a story of my Lancashire family.* Ramsbottom: Tower Press, 1970. 19-20th c.

Faraday

FARADAY, JOSEPH E. & FARADAY, MICHAEL ANTHONY. *The Faraday genealogy.* [ ]: privately published, 1967. Of Bolton le Sands, 17-20th c.

Farington

'Farington pedigree', *M.G.H.* **1**, 1868, 63. 16-17th c.

Farrer

FARRER, THOMAS CECIL, LORD. *Some Farrer memorials, being a selection from the papers of Thomas Henry, first Lord Farrer, 1819-1899, on various matters connected with his life, with notes relating to some branches of the family of Greystoneley, Ingleborough, Abinger, between 1610 and 1923.* G. Sherwood, 1923. Includes pedigrees, 17-20th c.

Fazakerley

See Hawarden

Feilden

ASSHETON, RALPH. *Pedigree of the family of Feilden of the County of Lancaster.* Mitchell & Hughes, 1879. 17-19th c.

WILSON, R.D.S. *The Feildens of Witton Park (the chronicles of a Lancashire family).* Blackburn: Borough of Blackburn Dept. of Recreation [198-?] Includes pedigrees, 16-20th c.

Fell

BARBER, HENRY. *Swarthmore Hall and its associations.* F. B. Kitto, [1872?] Fell family, 17th c.

FELL, JOHN. *The pedigree of Fell of Dalton Gate, Ulverston.* Kerby and Endean, 1882. Includes folded pedigree, 17-19th c.

WEBB, MARIA. *The Fells of Swarthmore Hall and their friends, with an account of their ancestor Anne Askew the martyr.* Philadelphia: H. Longstreth, 1896. 16-17th c.

'Fell family of Pennington in Furness', *C.F.H.S.N.* **59**, 1991, 20-22; **60**, 1991, 2-8. Pedigree, 16-18th c., with wills.

Fenwick

CHIPPINDALL, W.H. Fenwick of Burrow Hall in Lonsdale', *C.W.A.A.S.Tr.* N.S., **36**, 1936, 8-19. Includes folded pedigree, 18-20th c., and wills, etc.

Ferguson

'Family bibles', *M.G.* **27**(4), 1991, 67-8. Of the Ferguson, Brook and Hall families, 18-19th c.

Fergusson

See Cronshaw

Ferriar

'John Ferriar, M.D. of Manchester', *P.N.* **2**, 1882, 65-71 & 100-8. See also 127-8. Includes pedigree, 18-19th c.

Fielden

FISHWICK, HENRY. *A genealogical memorial of the family of Fielden of Todmorden, in the counties of York and Lancaster, with appendices of parish registers, wills, monumental inscriptions and original documents, together with notices of the family in Newark, in County of Nottingham, and in various parts of Lancashire and Yorkshire.* Mitchell and Hughes, 1884. Includes folded pedigree, 16-19th c.

FITTON, MICHAEL. 'Fielden of Bottomley, Todmorden', *L.* **11**(4), 1990, 27-33. Includes pedigree, 18-19th c.

Finch

FINCH, RICHARD NORMAN, & FINCH, EVELYN SHEILA. *Our Finch family and others, mainly from Worcestershire and Cambridgeshire, spreading to London and Lancashire, including a social and general history for each generation; also a short history of the churches used covering the years 1545-1993.* [ ]: the authors, 1993.

Fisher

See Dawes

Fleetwood

BAGLEY, JOHN JOSEPH. 'The Fleetwoods of Upholland', *L.C.A.S.* **58**, 1945-6, 35-57. Includes pedigrees, 16-18th c.

BUSS, R.W.H. *The ancestry of William Fleetwood, Bishop of St. Asaph and Ely, with a pedigree.* The author, 1926. Fleetwood of Upholland and London, includes folded pedigree, 17-18th c.

BUSS, ROBERT WOODWARD. *Fleetwood family records.* 7 pts. Privately printed, 1914-21. Of Lancashire and London, *etc.,* 1419th c.

RUDKIN, H.E. 'Fleetwood of Rossall', *Notes and queries* **172**, 1937, 276-81. Pedigree, 16-19th c., with wills of Richard Fleetwood of Rossall, 1708, and Margaret Fleetwood of Preston, 1719.

'Case concerning the estate of a family of Fleetwood of Prescott, A.D.1745', *L.C.A.N.* **1**, 1885, 160-5. 17-18th c., opinion of Counsel prepared in 1745.

Fleming

CHIPPINDALL, W.H. 'Early Flemings of Furness', *C.W.A.A.S.Tr.* N.S., **31**, 1931, 29-32. Includes pedigree, 12th c.

Folds

HALL, WILLIAM FOLDS. *The Folds of Daneshouse: a Burnley family and their home.* Newbury: the author, 1960. Includes pedigree, 16-17th c.
See also Haworth

Ford-Smith
See Cronshaw

Forster

FOSTER, JOSEPH. *A pedigree of the Forsters and Fosters of the north of England, and of some of the families connected with them.* Privately published, 1871. Detailed; includes pedigrees, medieval-19th c.

Froggatt
See Mort

Gale
See Braddyll

Gamon

BROXAP, HENRY. 'Some new facts concerning Thomas Deacon', *L.C.A.S.* **29**, 1911, 70-88. Includes pedigree of Gamon and Deacon, 18-19th c.

Gardner

GARDNER, JOAN M. 'A misleading marriage affidavit: the Gardners at Claughton, 1824', *L.* **10**(1), 1989, 12-14. Includes pedigree.

Garstang

GURNEY, GAMZU. *From generation to generation: the story of a Lancashire clan.* Research Publishing, 1970. Garstang family: includes pedigrees, 17-20th c.

Garth
See Hilliard

Gaskell
See Kay

Geldart
See Gildart

Gellibrand
See Hawarden

Gerard

GIBLIN, J.F. 'The Gerard family of Bryn and Ince, and the parish of Ss. Oswald and Edmund in Ashton-in-Makerfield', *N.W.C.H.* **17**, 1990, 1-17. Medieval-20th c.

Gilbert
See Royds

Gildart

GILDART, CHARLES, R. *The Gildart-Geldart families.* [Sierra Madra, California]: privately printed, 1962. Of Carlton, Yorkshire, Liverpool, Staffordshire, and the United States, 17-20th c.

Gillow

WHITEHEAD, M. 'The Gillows and their work in Georgian Lancaster', in HILTON, J.A., ed. *Catholic Englishmen: essays presented to the Rt. Rev. Brian Charles Foley, Bishop of Lancaster.* Wigan: North West Catholic History Society, 1984, 21-8.

Gladstone

CHECKLAND, S.G. *The Gladstones: a family biography, 1764-1851.* Cambridge: Cambridge University Press, 1971.

Gleave

BURGESS, JOHN. 'The Gleaves of St.Helens, a Methodist family', *Journal of the Lancashire and Cheshire branch of the Wesley Historical Society* 3(4), 1976, 67-72. 19-20th c.

Glynn

BEAZLEY, F.C. 'The pedigree of Glynn of Glynn, in the county of Cornwall, and of Liverpool, in the County Palatine of Lancaster', *Genealogist* N.S., **24**, 1908, 145-63. See also **25**, 1909, 266; **33**, 1917, 238-40. 15-19th c., includes wills.

Goad

GAYTHORPE, HARPER. 'The Goads of Furness', *Barrow Naturalist Field Club and Literary and Scientific Association proceedings &c.* **19**, 1906-10, 65-6. Brief note, 14-17th c.

Gorton

HIGGINS, JOHN. *The Gortons of Gorton and other places in Lancashire.* [ ], 1873. Reprinted as *The history of the Gorton family.* Mitre Press, [1931?] Chronological listing of births, marriages, deaths, and other events.

HIGSON, JOHN. 'The Gortons of Gorton and other places in Lancashire', *M.G.H.* N.S., **1**, 1874, 321-5 & 378-9. 16-19th c., brief biographical notes *etc.*

STONE, ELLIOT. 'Contribution to a Gorton genealogy', *New England historical and genealogical register* **51**, 1897, 199-200. 17th c.

Gradwell

CARTER, H.V. 'The Gradwells and the quest for Ann', *M.G.* **14**(1), 1978, 9-11. Medieval-19th c.

Grant

ELLIOT, W. HUME. *The country and church of the Cheeryble brothers.* Selkirk: G. Lewis & Son, 1893. Grant family, prototypes of the Cheeryble brothers in Dickens's *Nicholas Nickleby.*

ELLIOT, W.H. *The story of the Cheeryble Grants: from the Spey to the Irwell.* Manchester: Sherratt and Hughes, 1906. Grant family.

HAYHURST, T.H. *An appreciative estimate of the Grant Brothers of Ramsbottom (the 'brothers Cheeryble').* Bury: T. Crompton & Co., 1884.

See also Dinwiddie

Greenhalgh

FOX, BRENDA M. 'A Greenhalgh family of Bradshaw', *L.* **13**(1), 1992, 32-42. Includes pedigree, 18-20th c.

GREENHALGH, J.D. *Historical notes, being some account of the Greenhalgh family from early time, as pertaining to a foundation branch, known as the 'Brandlesome Order' ...* Bolton: Daily Chronicle Printing Works, 1877. Reprinted Research Publishing Co., [197-?]

GREENHALGH, JOSEPH DODSON. *Memoranda of the Greenhalgh family.* Bolton: T. Abbatt's Machine Printing Works, 1869. 18-19th c.

TOPHAM, M.M. 'The Greenhalgh family', *M.G.* **28**(3), 1992, 379. 17-19th c.

Greg

ROSE, MARY B. *The Gregs of Quarry Bank Mill: the rise and decline of a family firm, 1750-1914.* Cambridge: C.U.P., 1986. Includes pedigrees of Greg, 18-20th c., and Lightbody, 18-19th c.

FROW, E. & FROW, R. 'The Gregs of Styal: were they benevolent employers?' *Eccles and District History Society lectures* 1984-5, 73-87. 18-19th c.

Gregge

'Gregge and Holt families of Cheshire and Lancashire', *P.N.,* **4**, 1884, 237-8. Includes brief pedigree, 17-18th c.

Grelley

FARRER, WILLIAM. 'The Barony of Grelley', *H.S.L.C.* **53**; N.S., **17**, 1901, 23-58. Medieval.

KANDEL, EDWARD M. 'The Barons of Manchester', *Coat of arms* 4(113), 1980, 228-32. Includes pedigree, 12-16th c., of Grelley and De La Warre

WHATTON, WILLIAM ROBERT. *Observations on the armorial bearings of the town of Manchester, and on the descent of the baronial family of Grelley.* Manchester: the author, 1824. Includes medieval Grelley pedigree.

Griffies
See Roscoe

Grimshaw
BAKER, F. 'The Grimshaw family', *Transactions of the Halifax Antiquarian Society* 1945, 49-72. Of Brindle and Halifax, Yorkshire, 18-19th c.

Guest
MCALPINE, IAN. 'The Guest family of Prestwich, 1628-1850', *M.G.* 31(1), 1995, 23-8. To be continued. 17th c.

Haddock
GAMBLE, JOHN. *The descendants of John Haddock.* [ ], 1897. 19th c. pedigrees; of Ravenshead.

Hall
WEST, JAMES. 'The Halls of Knotty Ash', *L.F.H.* 15(1), 1993, 23. Extracts from family bible, early 19th c.
See also Ferguson

Halliwell
TRIGG, W.B. 'Pyke House, Littleborough', *Transactions of the Halifax Antiquarian Society* 1933, 71-7. Halliwell family, 16-18th c.

Hallmark
HINTON, JOHN. 'Hallmarks, ironmongers of Preston', *L.* 11(2), 1990, 41-4.

Halsall
See Rigby

Halsted
CHAPPLES, LESLIE. *Of Yeoman stock: the Halsteds of Rowley.* Farnham: R. Lewis-Jones, [1978]. 17-19th c.

Hamer
HAMER, GEOFFREY. *The history of Hamer: the origins of the name and a Lancashire family.* Bolton: the author, 1994. 14-20th c., includes extracts from parish register, census returns *etc.*

Hampson
HARPER, SANDRA. 'Hampsons, lost and found', *M.G.* 28(3), 1992, 7-9.

Hancock
PARKER, WILKINSON & PARTINGTON, S.W. 'Hancock family of Pendle', *L.C.A.S.,* 31, 1913, 131-7. 15-17th c.

Hardman
DEARDEN, JOHN. 'A Lancashire family, 4: the Hardman family of Little Carleton, Poulton le Fylde', *L.* 5(4), 1984, 17-19. Includes pedigree, 17-19th c.
FISHWICK, LIEUT. COL. 'Notes on the Hardman family', *H.S.L.C.* 42; N.S., 6, 1890, 77-80. 17th c.
DEARDEN, JOHN. 'Further researches into Hardman of Little Carleton', *L.* 8(1), 1987, 16-18. See also 8(2), 1987, 11. 16-18th c.
'The Hardman family of Manchester', *P.N.* 4, 1884, 167-70. See also 201-2, 225 & 240-42. 18-19th c.

Hargreaves
See Thursby

Harrison
AXON, ERNEST. 'Harrison Ainsworth's maternal ancestors', *L.C.A.S.* 29, 1911, 103-53. Harrison family; includes pedigree, 16-18th c. Also includes notes on Cooper of Dukinfield, Cheshire, and Swarbreck of Roseacre.
CRIPPS, WILFRED J. 'Pedigree of the family of Harrison', *M.G.H.* N.S., 4, 1884, 118-24. Of Lancashire, Middlesex, *etc.,* 16-19th c.
EARWAKER, J.P. *A Lancashire pedigree case, or, a history of the various trials for the recovery of the Harrison estates, from 1873 to 1886, together with a full account of the many forgeries and fraudulent entries in parish registers, marriage licence bonds &c., publicly exposed at the trial at Liverpool, May 25th to 28th 1886, with a pedigree of the Harrison family.* Warrington: Mackie & Co., 1887.

HARRISON, CUTHBERT WOODVILLE. *The Harrisons of Newton and Bankfield in Lancashire.* Exeter: William Pollard & Co., 1939. 16-20th c. Includes extensive extracts from original sources, especially the parish register of Kirkham St. Michael.

HARRISON, M.J. *The early history of the Harrisons of Freckleton, Co. Lancashire.* [ ]: Privately published, 1922. Includes folded pedigree, 16-18th c., and many extracts from original sources.

'The ancestry of Cuthbert Harrison', *H.S.L.C.* **93**, 1941, 12-56. 16-17th c.

See also Ainsworth

Hart
SWAIN, MARGARET. 'A Lancashire family, 11: Hart of Anderton, Ashton-in-Makerfield, & Hindley', *L.* **7**(3), 1986, 18-29. Includes pedigree, 17-20th c.

Hasell
SCHOFIELD, E.M., & SCHOFIELD, M.M. 'A good fortune and a good wife: the marriage of Christopher Hasell of Liverpool, merchant, 1765', *H.S.L.C.* **138**, 1989, 85-111. Includes pedigree, 18th c.

Hastings
See Woodcock

Hawarden
WALSH, V. HUSSEY. 'The pedigree of the late Henry Hawarden-Gellibrand-Fazakerley and the descent to him of Fazakerley Hall, Gellibrand Hall, and Lower House in Widnes', *Genealogist* N.S., **33**, 1917, 178-83 & 223-37. Includes pedigrees, 13-20th c., of Fazakerley, Gellibrand and Hawarden.

Hawkins
See Cronshaw

Haworth
'Sayings and doings of Parson Folds: the Haworth family', in BARTON, B.T., ed. *Historical gleanings of Bolton and District [first series].* Bolton: Daily Chronicle Office, 1881, 278-86. 18th c.

Haydock
GILLOW, JOSEPH. *The Haydock papers: a glimpse into English Catholic life under the shade of persecution and in the dawn of freedom.* Burns & Oates, 1838. Haydock family, 15-19th c.

Hayward
'The Hayward family of Warrington', *L.G.* **2**, 1877, 29-30, 18-19th c.

Healiss
HARRISON, MONA C. 'A Lancashire lad?', *L.* **3**(4), 1980, 14-15. Healiss family; includes pedigree, 19-20th c.

Heape
HEAPE, CHARLES & HEAPE, RICHARD. *Records of the family of Heape of Heape, Staley, Saddleworth and Rochdale, from circa 1170 to 1905.* Rochdale: Aldine Press, 1905. Includes pedigrees (some folded) and many extracts from original sources.

Hemming
See Cowell

Hendy
See Slone

Hengler
TURNER, JOHN M. 'Historical Hengler's Circus: a family historian's approach', *L.F.H.* **4**(3), 1982, 48-54. Includes Hengler pedigree, 19-20th c.

Henry
FARRAR, W.V., FARRAR, KATHLEEN R., & SCOTT, E.L. 'The Henrys of Manchester', *Ambix: the journal of the Society for the History of Alchemy and Chemistry* **20**, 1973, 183-208; **21**, 1974, 179-228; **23**, 1976, 27-52; **24**, 1977, 1-26. 18-19th c.

Henshaw
'A sketch of the life of Hon. Joshua Henshaw, with brief notices of other members of the Henshaw family, *New England historical and genealogical register* **22**, 1868, 105-15. Includes pedigree of Henshaw of Lancashire, 17-19th c.

Henthorn

RATHBONE, PETER. 'The Henthorns: a Lancashire family', *M.G.* **26**(1), 1990, 19-23.

Hesketh

PROCTER, W.G. 'The manor of Rufford and the ancient family of the Heskeths', *H.S.L.C.* **59**; N.S., **23**, 1907, 93-118. 13-19th c.

PROCTOR, W.G. 'Notes on the Hesketh pedigree', *H.S.L.C.* **62**; N.S., **26**, 1910, 58-66. Medieval-17th c. Of Rufford.

The genealogye of the worshipful and auncient familie of the Heskaythes of Ruffourd in Lancashire, copied from the original roll in the possession of Sir Thomas George Fermor-Hesketh of Rufford, Bart., together with the Hesketh pedigrees from the Visitations of Lancashire, 1613, 1664, etc. Taylor and Co., 1869.

'The genealogye of the worshippful and auncient familie of the Heskaythes of Ruffourd in Lancashire', *M.G.H.* **2**, 1876, 140-54. Medieval-18th c.

Heywood

HEYWOOD, NATHAN. 'Captain Peter Heywood', *L.C.A.S.* **9**, 1891, 135-46. Includes extensive folded pedigree, 13-18th c.

Heywood

JAMES, RICHARD. *Iter Lancastrense: a poem written A.D. 1636 ...,* ed. Thomas Corser. C.S. **7**, 1845. Includes folded pedigree of Heywood of Heywood, 14-18th c., also of James of the Isle of Wight, 15-16th c.

Hidden

'Families of Hidden's and Idden's in Lancashire', *M.G.* Winter 1973/4, 5-11; Spring 1975, 8-9.

Hide '

See Urm(e)stone

Higginbottom

The Higginbottom family bulletin. Canterbury: Frank Higginbottom, 1970-81. Includes many articles of Lancashire and Cheshire interest not otherwise listed here.

'In search of Higginbottoms', *M.G.* **29**(4) 1993, 37-8. Description of the collection of Higginbottom genealogical materials held at Stockport Local Studies Library.

Hilliard

MACKEY, MARJORIE & FRANK. 'A Lancashire family 28: the Hilliards and the Garths of Halton, Lancaster and Liverpool', *L.* **11**(4), 1990, 22-6. Includes pedigree, 17-20th c.

Hills

See Dunster

Hindle

'A Lancashire family: Hindle of Darwen', *L.* **9**(2), 1988, 32-41. Includes pedigree, 19th c.

Hodgkinson

'Evidences of the family of Hodgkinson of Preston', *P.N.* **4**, 1884, 163-7, 188-90 & 221-3. 16th c. deeds, mainly concerning Preston. Also includes pedigree, 16-18th c.

Hoghton

ABRAM, W.A. 'Descent of Hoghtons of Hoghton Tower from Lady Godiva', *L.C.A.N.* **1**, 1885, 19-21. 13-14th c.

Holcroft

CROFTON, H.T. 'Dumplington and the Holcrofts', *L.C.A.S.* **24**, 1906, 21-45. Includes folded pedigree, 17-18th c.

RYLANDS, JOHN PAUL. *Notes on the families of Holcroft, of Holcroft, Co. Lancaster; Holcroft of Vale Royal, Co. Chester, Holcroft of Hurst, Co. Lancaster, Holcroft of East Ham, Co. Essex; Holcroft of Balderton, Co. Nottinghamshire, Holcroft of Basingstoke, Co. Hampshire, etc., with an account of their arms.* Leigh: Josiah Rose, 1877. Medieval-18th c.

WARD, JOHN CAMERON. 'Holcroft of Holcroft, Vale Royal, Dumplington & Burscough', *L.* **8**(2), 1987, 28-35. Medieval-19th c.

Holland

HOLLAND, BERNARD. *The Lancashire Hollands.* John Murray, 1917. Includes many pedigrees, medieval-19th c.

IRVINE, WM. FERGUSSON, ed. *A history of the family of Holland of Mobberley and Knutsford in the County of Chester, with some account of the family of Holland of Upholland and Denton in the County of Lancaster, from materials collected by the late Edgar Swinton Holland.* Edinburgh: Ballantyne Press, 1902. Includes deed abstracts, extracts from parish registers, folded pedigrees, 13-19th c., etc.

L., W. 'Family of Holland', *Local notes and gleanings from the Manchester Guardian* **120**, 1876, 1-2. Medieval.

See also Dukinfield

Hollingworth

See Wild

Holloway

See Cronshaw

Holme

See Woodcock

Holt

BURROWS, CONSTANCE. 'Holt of Tottington: from a family bible', *L.* **10**(4), 1989, 28-9. Includes pedigree, 18-20th c.

HOLLEDGE, MARION. 'A Lancashire family, 19: Holt of Standish and the City of London', *L.* **9**(3), 1988, 19-28. See also **9**(4), 1988, 14. Includes pedigree, 16-18th c.

HOLLEDGE, MARION. 'Sir John Holt: likely descent of a 17th century Lord Chief Justice from Grizlehurst Holts', *L.* **10**(3), 1989, 18-21. Includes suggested pedigree.

'Edward Holt's family bible (1760-1840)', *M.G.* Autumn 1973, 11-12.

'A brief history of the Holts, inhabiting Stubley Hall, near Littleborough, and Castleton Hall, south of Rochdale, for nearly three centuries', *Family History Society of Cheshire [journal]* **8**(3), 1979, 13-15. 16-18th c.

See also Gregge

Hornby

ABRAM, W.A. *Members of the Hornby family who have served Blackburn in Parliament.* Manchester: Falkner, 1892.

MOSEY, HELEN. 'A brief history of the family of Rachel Hornby', *Catholic Ancestor* **4**(1), 1992, 20-23. Includes pedigree, 17-20th c.

See also Cowell

Horrocks

G., J.D. 'Supplementary sketch on James Horrocks and his family at Bradshaw', in BARTON, B.T., ed. *Historical gleanings of Bolton and District [first series].* Bolton: Daily Chronicle Office 1881, 264-7. 17-19th c.

Horrox

HORROX, CONRAD. 'A Horrox family', *M.G.* **22**(1), 1986, 40-41. 18-20th c., of Manchester.

Horsfall

See Tobin

Hoskins

See Master

Hough

See Liverpool

Houghton

HOUGHTON, B.A. 'The Houghton family: circumstances and Catholicism in seventeenth-century Halewood', *N.W.C.H.* **11**, 1984, 5-7.

Howarth

HOWARTH, ARTHUR J. 'A Howarth family of Roughlee and Burnley', *L.* **11**(4), 1990, 33-7. 18-19th c.

Howorth

'Howorth pedigree', *M.G.H.* **1**, 1868, 104. 16-17th c.

Hoyle

HARRISON, GEORGE G. 'Hoyle/Kenyon: summary of research', *L.* **14**(4), 1993, 24-30. 18-19th c.

KELLY, MARY. 'A Lancashire family, 7: Hoyle of Bacup in the Rossendale Valley of Lancashire', *L.* 6(3), 1985, 17-19. Includes pedigree, 18-19th c.
SIMPSON, JOHN. 'A Lancashire family, 29: Hoyle of Haslingden and Peru', *L.* 12(1), 1991, 23-8. Includes pedigree, 18-20th c.

Hudson
See Royds

Hulme
OWEN, J. 'Hulme and Strettle families', *A.N.Q.* 3, 1883, 146-7. Of Manchester and Mobberley, Cheshire; includes parish register extracts, 16-18th c.

Hulton
'The Hultons of Hulton, and the Orrells of Turton', in BARTON, B.T., ed. *Historical gleanings of Bolton and District [third series].* Bolton: Daily Chronicle Office, 1883, 267-75. Medieval-17th c.
See also Ashawe

Hurst
LOWE, A.E.LAWSON. 'The family of Hurst of Hurst, in the parish of Ashton-under-Lyne, Co. Lancaster', *Genealogist* 5, 1881, 139-41.

Idden
See Hidden

Inglesent
DANIELS, PHILIP H. 'Hearth tax assessments and finding a lost family', *North Cheshire family historian* 4(1), 1977, 16-18. Inglesent family of Monyash, Derbyshire, and Manchester.

Ireland
IRVINE, WM. FERGUSSON. 'The origin of the Irelands of Hale', *H.S.L.C.* 52; N.S., 16, 1900, 139-46. Medieval.
See also Blackburne

James
See Heywood

Jenkinson
See Mellard

Job
JOB, ROBERT BROWN. *John Job's family: a story of his ancestors and successors and their business connections with Newfoundland and Liverpool, 1730-1953.* 2nd ed. St.Johns, Newfoundland: Telegram Printing, 1954. Also of Devon.

Johnson
WESTBY, G. 'Leaves from family bibles, no. 27. Johnson; Smaltham', *Pedigree register* 3, 1913-16, 87-8. 19-20th c.

Jones
AXON, ERNEST. 'John Jones and Edmund Jones, vicars of Eccles, 1611-1662', *L.C.A.S.* 36, 1918, 65-77.

Jordan
JORDAN, THOS. L. 'Oak Hall, Cross Lane, Salford, and the Jordan family', *P.N.* 4, 1884, 140-2. 18th c.

Kay
KAY, KENNETH. *The chronicles of the family of Kay of Lancashire from the XIV to the XXth century.* Sumter, South Carolina: Kay Family Association, 1992. Originally published 1909. The 1992 edition includes SPEARMAN, FRANK. *The English heritage of James Kay of the colony of Virginia.*
RAMSDEN, G.M. *A record of the Kay family of Bury, Lancashire, in the 17th and 18th centuries with notes on the families of Gaskell, Mangnall, Darbishire.* Horsham: the author, 1978.
SCHOLES, JAS. C. 'The Kays of Turton Tower', in BARTON, B.T., ed. *Historical gleanings of Bolton and District [second series.]* Bolton: Daily Chronicle Office, 1882, 103-6. 18-19th c.
See also Melladew

Kelsall
BEEDEN, JULIA M. 'Kelsall: a Quaker family', *Over Wyre historical journal* 4, 1986-7, 12-14; 5, 1988-9, 18-19; 6, 1990-91, 25-9. 17-19th c.

Kenney
HALL, JOHN RAYMOND. 'Three generations of a Kenney family;', *M.G.* 22(1), 1986, 20-23.

Kenyon

MUIR, AUGUSTUS. *The Kenyon tradition: the history of James Kenyon & Son Ltd., 1664-1964.* Cambridge: W. Heffer & Sons, 1964. History of the family business.
MORIARTY, G. ANDREWS. 'Further light on Roger Kenyon III', *Genealogists' magazine* 11, 1953, 409-11. 18th c.
See also Liverpool and Rigby

Kershaw

ABRAM, W.A. 'Ancient Lancashire families IV: the Kershaws of Rochdale and of Heskin Hall in Ecclestone', *L.C.A.N.* 2, 1886, 132-40. 16-18th c., includes will of Alexander Kershaw, 1788.
'Kershaw family records', *M.G.* 11(2), 1975, 11. From a prayer book, 18-19th c. Of Cheadle.

Kight

SIMMONS, J. 'The Kights of North England', *M.G.* 14(4), 1978, 97-100. 18-19th c.

Kirkby

COWPER, H.S. 'The homes of the Kirkbys of Kirkby Ireleth', *C.W.A.A.S.Tr.* 13, 1895, 269-86. Includes pedigree, 15-16th c.
COWPER, H.S. 'The Kirkbys of Kirkby-in-Furness in the seventeenth century, illustrated by their portraits', *C.W.A.A.S.Tr.* N.S., 6, 1906, 97-127. See also 21, 1921, 275-6. Includes pedigree.
C., W.O. 'The Kirkbys of Kirkby Ireleth: a Cavalier family', *Genealogical magazine* 3, 1899-1900, 494-7 & 531-3. Medieval-18th c.

Knight

See Whiteside

Knowles

SCHOLES, JAS. C. *Genealogy of the Knowles family, of Edgworth, Quarlton, Little Bolton and Swinton.* [Bolton]: Privately printed, 1886. Reprinted from the *Bolton journal.* 16-19th c.

Lace

See Roscoe

Laithwaite

LAITHWAITE, GILBERT, SIR. *The Laithwaites: some records of a Lancashire family.* Rev. ed. Karachi: privately printed, 1961. Medieval-17th c., many extracts from wills, deeds, parish registers, *etc.*
See also Cooper

Landless

WHITTAKER, GLADYS. *The family of Landless.* Nelson: the author, 1970. Of Scotland, Northumberland and Nelson, Lancashire.

Lang

See Cronshaw

Langley

KEELAN, JOHN. 'The Langley family, the Ainsworths, and Middleton manor', *Family history* 13(102); N.S., 78, 1985, 265-6. Medieval.
KELLY, CHRISTINE. 'The Langley family: Sir Geoffrey de Langley, founder of the Langley family', *Family history* 13(100); N.S., 76, 157-93. Includes pedigree, 13-17th c.
'Langley pedigree', *M.G.H.* 2nd series. 2, 1888, 273-83, 305-9 & 337-9; 3, 1890, 75-80, 141-4, 158-60 & 169-72. Of Shropshire, Glamorganshire, Warwickshire, Lancashire, Yorkshire, Kent and London; 13-19th c.

Langstroth

TODD, ANDREW A. 'The Langstroths of Horton-in-Ribblesdale and Elton', *L.* 6(1), 1985, 30-35. 18-20th c.

Langton

LANGTON, ANNE. *The story of our family.* Manchester: Thos. Sowler & Co., 1881. Langton family of Kirkham and Blythe Hall. 19th c.

Lathom

BERRY, R.J.A. 'An enquiry into the supposed connection of the founder of Peter Lathom's Charity with the Lathoms of Parbold', *H.S.L.C.* 97, 1945, 85-100. Includes folded pedigree, 13-19th c.
'Lathom pedigree', *M.G.H.* 1, 1868, 161. 17th c.

Launder
See Master

Laurence
'Laurence pedigree', *M.G.H.* **1**, 1868, 199-211.
Of Lancashire, Dorset, Cambridgeshire,
Somerset, Gloucestershire, London and
Buckinghamshire; medieval-17th c.

Law
JACKSON, WM. 'The Laws of Buck Crag in
Cartmel, and of Bampton', *C.W.A.A.S.Tr.*,
2, 1876, 264-76. Bampton, Westmorland.
Includes folded pedigree, 16-18th c., with
wills.

Lawrence
LAWRENCE, R.G. 'Lawrence of Ashton, Co.
Lancaster, *Herald and genealogist* **8**, 1874,
210-19. Medieval.
See also Paulet

Leech
LEECH, E.B. *The Leech family of Ashton-
under-Lyne, Lancashire.* Manchester:
privately printed, 1924. 16-19th c.

Leigh
PINK, W.D. 'The Stoneleigh peerage case',
Genealogist magazine **4**, 1900-1901, 398-9.
Leigh family, 17-18th c., of Haigh,
17-18th c.-
See also Willoughby and Woodcock

Lewis
AXON, WILLIAM E.A. 'Who was Mistress
Joyce Lewis of Manchester?' *L.C.A.S.* **4**,
1886, 145-8. 16th c.

Lightbody
See Grey

Lindsay
See Bradshaigh

Lingard
AINSWORTH, RICHARD. *The Lingards of
Huncoat and their descendants.*
Accrington: Wardleworth, 1930. 17-19th c.
'Whose family', *North Cheshire family
historian* **4**(4), 1977, 116. Extracts from
the bible of the Lingard family, of
Manchester and Stockport, Cheshire.

Littledale
See Royds

Liverpool
ELTON, JOHN. 'William the son of Adam,
first recorded mayor of Liverpool',
H.S.L.C. **55-6**; N.S., **19-20**, 1903-4, 114-32.
Sometimes referred to as 'de Liverpool'.
14th c., includes pedigrees of Kenyon with
Almorice, Aynesargh, and Hough with Del
Crosse.

Livesey
LIVESEY, JOHN. 'Liveseys of Sidebright, in
Rishton, Lancashire', *Lincolnshire notes
and queries* **20**, 1929, 121-4; **21**, 1931, 13(f).
Includes folded pedigree, 15-18th c.

Lloyd
'The geonealgeye of Henrey Lloyd ali's
Rossindall of Cheyme in the com. of
Surrey, esq.', *M.G.H.* **2**, 1876, 277-9. Of
Rossendale, Derbyshire and Cheam,
Surrey; medieval-16th c.

Lomas
See Lomax

Lomax
LOMAX, JOHN B. 'On the origin of the
Lomax/Lomas surname', *L.* **10**(1), 1989,
16-19.

Longford
LONGFORD, WILLIAM WINGFIELD. 'Some
notes on the family history of Nicholas
Longford, sheriff of Lancashire in 1413',
H.S.L.C. **86**, 1934, 47-71. Also of
Derbyshire.

Longmoor
See also Wild

Longworth
JONES, PHILIP E. *A short history of the
Longworth and Almond families of
Belmont, Lancashire.* [Sutton in Ashfield:
the author,] 1970. 19th c., brief pamphlet.

Lord
TODD, ANDREW. 'A Lancashire family, 16:
Lord of Broadclough, Bacup', *L.* **8**(4),
1987, 28-34. 16-18th c., includes pedigree.

TODD, A.A. 'A Lancashire family, 15: Lord of Kearsley, Farnworth, Ainsworth, Bolton & Tyldesley', *L.* 8(3), 1987, 20-32. Includes pedigree, 18-19th c.

WARD, JOHN CAMERON. 'Lord of Bacup, Greave in Langfield, Manchester, and Australia: the Australian gene', *L.* 10(4), 1989, 37-40. 19-20th c.

Lowe

TODD, ANDREW A. 'A Lancashire family, 3: Lowe of Heaton and Hinde', *L.* 5(3), 1984, 16-20, Includes pedigree, 18-19th c.

TODD, ANDREW. 'Notes on sources, 33: the Bury Savings Bank archive, 2: a case study: Lowe of Elton', 11(1), 1990, 30-34. Includes pedigree 18-19th c.

See also Cooper

Lowther

BECKETT, J.V. 'The Lowthers at Holker: marriage, inheritance and debt in the fortunes of an eighteenth-century landowning family', *H.S.L.C.* 127, 1978, 47-64.

OWEN, HUGH. *The Lowther family: eight hundred years of a family of ancient gentry and worship.* Chichester: Phillimore, 1990. Of Cumberland and Yorkshire, as well as of Holker, Lancashire. Includes pedigrees, 12-20th c.

Loxham

BARLOW, ANGELA. 'A Lancashire family, 21: Loxham of Longton', *L.* 10(1), 1989, 25-36. Includes pedigree, 17-19th c.

Lucas

'The Lucas dossier', *M.G.* Summer 1974, 14-15. 16-19th c.

Lumb

See Clarke

Lymme

See Statham

Lynd

See Lynn

Lynn

LYNN, G.H. 'Messing about with Lynns', *M.G.* 29(1), 1993, 16-18; 30(1), 1994, 25-8. 18-19th c. Lynn or Lynd family.

McClure

DUNLOP, A. *Memorabilia of the McClures.* Salisbury: M. O. Collins (Pvt.), 1972. Includes pedigrees, 18-20th c.

Macfarlane

DEARDEN, GORDON. 'A Macfarlane family of Preston and Perth', *M.G.,* 26(3), 1990, 33-7. 18-19th c.

Machell

COCKERILL, TIMOTHY. 'The Machell and Remington families of Aynsome, Cartmel', *C.W.A.A.S.Tr.* N.S., 89, 1989, 263-8. Includes pedigrees, 18-19th c.

Macrae

MACRAE, DAVID. 'The Macraes of Barwood Lee', *L.* 13(2), 1992, 30-38. Includes pedigree, 19-20th c.

MACRAE, DAVID. 'McRae's of Barwood Lee', *M.G.* 28(3), 1992, 47-50. Includes pedigree, 18-20th c.

Maghull

DAWSON-DUFFIELD, REV. 'Maghull of Maghull: memoranda from the registers of the parish church of Sephton, Lancashire', *M.G.H.* 2, 1876, 303. 17-18th c.

Mangnall

See Kay

Marcroft

MARCROFT, WILLIAM. *The Marcroft family.* Manchester: John Heywood, 1886. 19th c.

Mark(e)

YARMER, JOHN. *Genealogy of the family of Mark, or Marke, County of Cumberland; pedigree and arms of the Bowscale branch of the family, from which is descended John Mark, esquire, now residing at Greystoke, West Didsbury, near Manchester ...* Manchester: Palmer, Howe & Co., 1898. Includes folded pedigree, 17-20th c.

Markland

BAGLEY, J.J. 'Matthew Markland, a Wigan merchant: the manufacture and sale of Lancashire textiles in the reigns of Elizabeth I and James I', *L.C.A.S.* **68**, 1958, 45-68. Includes pedigree, 16-17th c.

BOYD, ARNOLD W. 'The Markland family deeds and papers', *L.C.A.S.* **47**, 1930-31, 27-57. Includes pedigree, 16-20th c.

Marriner

CORBISHLEY, A. 'In search of the Marriners', *North Cheshire family historian* **6**(1), 1979, 8-11. Marriner family of Manchester and Liverpool, 19th c.

Marsden

MARSDEN, BENJAMIN ANDERTON, MARSDEN, JAMES ASPINALL, & MARSDEN, ROBERT SYDNEY. *Genealogical memoirs of the family of Marsden: their ancestors and descent traced from public records, wills and other documents, and from private sources of information hitherto unrecorded.* Birkenhead: E. Griffith & Son, 1914. Medieval-19th c.

Marshall

'Pedigree of Marshall of Urswick, Hadham, Blewbury, Bosbury, etc., *Genealogist* **5**, 1881, 125-31. Hadham, Hertfordshire; Blewbury, Berkshire; Bosbury, Herefordshire; includes pedigree, 16-17th c., and wills of John and William Marshall, 1646 and 1676.

Marton

SMITH, RODNEY J. *The Capernwray story.* Capernwray: Capernwray Hall, 1965, Marton family, 17-20th c.

Mascy

TEMPEST, ARTHUR CECIL, MRS. 'The descent of the Mascys of Rixton in the County of Lancaster (from original documents)', *H.S.L.C.* **39**; N.S., **3**, 1887, 59-158. Includes pedigree, 14-18th c.

Master

MASTER, GEORGE STREYNSHAM. *Some notices of the family of Master, of East Langdon and Yotes in Kent, New Hall and Croston in Lancashire, and Barrow Green in Surrey, with appendices of abstracts of parish registers, monumental inscriptions, original documents and wills, together with notices of the families of Streynsham, Wightman, Launder, Hoskins and Whalley, now represented by that of Master.* Mitchell & Hughes, 1874. Includes folded pedigree, 18-19th c. Yotes is in Mereworth, Kent.

Mather

MATHER, HORACE E. *The lineage of Rev. Richard Mather.* Hartford, Connecticut: Case, Lockwood & Brainard Company, 1890, Mather family, originally of Winwick, but late of the United States, 16-19th c.

Mathias

See Cooper

Mawdesley

ABRAM, W.A. 'Ancient Lancashire families, I: the Mawdesleys of Mawdesley', *L.C.A.N.* **1**, 1885, 143-9. 14-18th c.

'Mawdesley of Orrell and Longport, Staffordshire: a nineteenth-century family history', *L.* **6**(1), 1985, 14-15. See also **6**(4), 1985, 13. 18-19th c.

M'Connell

M'CONNEL, D.C. *Facts and traditions collected for a family record.* Edinburgh: Ballantyne and Company, 1861. M'Connell family of Manchester, originally of Scotland; 17-19th c.

Meadowcroft

See Royds

Meakin

See Cronshaw

Melladew

'The Rev. Roger Kay: some of the founders' kin', *Bury and Rossendale historical review* **2**, 1910-11, 25-7. Notes on the Melladew family, 18-19th c., who were related to Kay.

Mellard

READE, ALLEYNE LYELL. *The Mellards & their descendants, including the Bibbys of Liverpool, with memoirs of Dinah Maria Mulock and Thomas Mellard Reade.* Arden Press, 1915. Of Newcastle under Lyme, Staffordshire, and Liverpool, *etc.* Includes pedigrees, 18-19th c., with extracts from parish registers and monumental inscriptions. Also includes notes on the Jenkinson and Bucknall families.

Melling

DICKINSON, FLORENCE. 'The Mellings of Rainhill', *H.S.L.C.* **121**, 1969, 59-75. 18-19th c.

Middleton

DEAN, JOHN. 'The ancient lords of Middleton', *L.C.A.S.* **15**, 1897, 122-74. Middleton family, medieval. Includes pedigree.

FARRER, WILLIAM. 'The family of Middleton of Middleton, in Salford Hundred', *L.C.A.S.* **17**, 1899, 32-47. Medieval; includes pedigree.

'Middleton of Leighton', *L.C.A.S.* **8**, 1890, 38. Pedigree, 14-19th c. Leighton is in Warton, Lancs.

See also Simpson.

Mills

WALLS, SHIRLEY. 'The Mills family and early industry in Heywood', *L.* **11**(2), 1990, 32-5. See also **11**(3), 1990, 17. 19th c.

Milne

See Crompton

Molineux

MOLINEUX, GISBORNE. *Memoir of the Molineux family.* J.S.Virtue and Co., 1882. Of Sefton, Haughton, Nottinghamshire, Staffordshire, Sussex, and Ireland, includes pedigrees, medieval-19th c.

Molyneaux

GIBLIN J.F. 'The Molyneaux family and the missions at Scholes Hall and Our Lady's, Portico', *N.W.C.H.* **21**, 1994, 1-13. Medieval-18th c., also includes lists of clergy, 19-20th c.

See also Royds and Stanley

Monks

CROSS, M.C. 'Monks family bible', *M.G.* **18**(2), 1982, 47. 18-19th c.

Montgomery

H. 'The family of De Montgomery', *P.N.* **1**, 1881, 185-7. Medieval; includes pedigree.

Moon

SHAW, R. CUNLIFFE. *Yeomen, craftsmen, merchants: the Moons of Amounderness and Leylandshire.* Preston: W. Watson & Co., 1963, 17-19th c.

Moore

HONE, JOSEPH. *The Moores of Moore Hall.* Jonathan Cape, 1939. 18-20th c.

STEWART-BROWN, RONALD. 'Moore of Bankhall', *H.S.L.C.* **63**, N.S., **27**, 1911, 92-118. 13-18th c.

Morley

MORLEY, KENNETH C. *Some Morleys of South West Lancashire: a genealogy.* Bootle: Print Origination, 1978. 17-20th c., includes folded pedigrees.

Mort

'The families of Mort, Sutton and Froggatt, lords of the manor of Astley, and the family of Plungeon of Manchester, Co. Lancaster, *P.N.,* **3**, 1883, 249-55. Includes pedigrees, 16-19th c.

Mosley

AXON, ERNEST. 'Mosley family: memoranda of Oswald and Nicholas Mosley of Ancoats from the Manchester Sessions ms. in the Free Reference Library, Manchester', *Chetham miscellanies* N.S., **1**. C.S., N.S., **47**, 1902. Includes pedigree, 16-17th c.

MOSLEY, SIR OSWALD. *Family memoirs.* Rolleston Hall: Privately published, 1849. Mosley family, 16-19th c.

Moss

'Ashton Moss', *M.G.* **13**(3), 1977, 65-6. Moss family baptism, 1788-98, in Ashton under Lyne, St. Michael's register.

Mulock

See Mellard

Nelson

'Nelson pedigrees as given in the visitations of Lancashire', *Genealogical magazine* 1, 1897-8, 657-8. 16-17th c.

Nicholson

NICHOLSON, FRANCIS. *Memorials of the family of Nicholson, of Blackshaw, Dumfriesshire, Liverpool and Manchester,* ed. Ernest Axon. Kendal: Titus Wilson and Son, 1928. Includes folded pedigree, 17-20th c.

Nisbet

INGLIS, JOHN A. 'The Nisbets of Carfin ...', *M.G.H.,* 5th series, 2, 1916-17, 44-52. 17-20th c.

Noblet, *etc.*

NOBLIT, JOHN HYNDMAN. *Genealogical collections relating to the families of Noblet, Noblat, Noblot and Noblets of France; Noblet and Noblett of Great Britain, Noblit and Noblitt of America, with some particular account of William Noblit ...* [Philadelphia]: Ferris & Leah, 1906. 17-19th c.

Normansell

'Normansell: an account of the family in Manchester', *M.G.* 18(3), 1982, 75-7. 18-19th c., includes pedigree.

Norres

ORMEROD, GEORGE. *A memoir on the Lancashire house of Le Noreis or Norres and its Speke branch in particular, with notices of its connexion with military transactions at Flodden, Edinburgh, and Musselburgh.* Liverpool: T. Brakell, 1850. Includes pedigrees, medieval-19th c.

ORMEROD, GEORGE. 'A memoir of the Lancashire house of Le Noreis or Norres, and on its Speke branch in particular, &c., with notices of its connexion with military transactions at Flodden, Edinburgh and Musselburgh', *H.S.L.C.* 2, 1850, 138-82. See also 3, 1851, 77-8. Includes pedigree, 13-16th c.

'Genealogical declaration respecting the family of Norres, written by Sir William Norres of Speke, Co. Lancaster, in the year 1563, accompanied by an abstract of ancient charters', *Topographer and genealogist* 2, 1853, 357-83.

Norris

See Bradshaigh

Nunn

'Nunn of Stonham Earl, Co. Suffolk, now of Ardwick, Co. Lancaster, and Lawton, Co. Chester', *M.G.H.* 2nd series, 2, 1888, 89. 18-19th c.

Nuttall

See Cronshaw

Nutter

FARRER, T.C. 'A key pedigree: Nutter of Reedley, Pendle, Lancashire', *Genealogists magazine* 1(1), 1925, 15-18. 17-18th c.

O'Garr

'The O'Garrs (O'Gara's) of Manchester', *M.G.* Summer 1972, 1316. 19-20th c.

Ogle

'Ogle of Roby', *H.S.L.C.* 75; N.S., 39, 1924, 260. Brief note, 17th c.

Okill

W., T.L.O. 'The Okills of Grappenhall, Warrington and Liverpool', *Cheshire sheaf* 3rd series, 9, 1913, 8-9 & 11-12. See also 12, 1917, 33-4. 17-18th c.

Openshaw

OPENSHAW, JOSEPH T., ed. *The Openshaw pedigree, together with a portion of the Ormerod pedigree shewing the connection between the two families.* Bury: Times Office, 1893. Medieval-19th c.

Orm

LATHAM, R.G. 'Upon the Orms of Lancashire in the twelfth century, and Orm the writer of the *Ormulum',* *H.S.L.C.,* 29; 3rd series, 5, 1877, 91-104.

Ormerod

ORME, J.E. 'The ancestry of George Ormerod, (1785-1873), historian of Cheshire', *M.G.* 30(4), 1994, 7-13. 17-19th c.

ORMEROD, E.A. *Eleanor Ormerod, LL.D.,
economic entomologist: autobiography and
correspondence,* ed. Robert Wallace. John
Murray, 1904. Includes genealogical notes.
See also Openshaw

Orrell
ORRELL, TERENCE ANTHONY DAVID.
History of the house of Orrell. Kettering:
David Green Printers, 1990. Includes
pedigrees, medieval-17th c. Also of
Cheshire and other counties.

Osbaldestone
LONGFORD, W.W. 'Some notes on the family
of Osbaldestone', *H.S.L.C.* **87**, 1935, 59-85.
Medieval-19th c.

Outlaw
SHONE, KEITH. 'Legend of the Outlaw
family', *M.G.* **23**(1), 1987, 46-8. 19th c.

Park
BERTHON, RAYMOND TINNE. 'Park of
Liverpool', *Pedigree register* **2**, 1910-13,
110-11. 18-19th c.

Parker
DUKE, J.E. 'Letter from Ulverston',
C.F.H.S.N., **53**, 1989, 8-11. Letter from
George Parker, 1824, with Parker
pedigree, 18-19th c.
See also Paulet

Parkinson
See Whiteside

Parkinson
AINSWORTH, RICHARD. *History of the
Parkinson family of Lancashire: their
genealogy, traditions, folk lore, and
associations.* Accrington: Wardlesworth,
1936. 13-20th c., includes folded
pedigrees.
AINSWORTH, RICHARD. *The Parkinson
family of Lancashire: a historical sketch.*
Accrington: Wardlesworth, 1932. Lecture
to L.C.A.S., medieval-19th c.
TODD, ANDREW A. 'Parkinson of
Oswaldtwistle and New Zealand', *L.* **7**(3),
1986, 37-42. See also **8**(4), 1987, 21-2.
Includes pedigree, 19-20th c.

Parr
P., H.H. 'Early pedigrees of the Parr family',
Topographer and genealogist **3**, 1858,
352-60. 14-16th c., of Westmorland,
Lancashire and Cheshire.
'Parr, Co. Lancaster', *The Patrician* **3**, 1847,
106-7. Parr family, 14-17th c.

Partington
HIRST, RITA. 'The I.G.I. and illegitimate
births: Partington of Heap Bridge',
L. **10**(4), 1989, 32-3. Includes pedigree,
19th c.

Paulet
FRANKLYN, CHARLES A.H. *A genealogical
history of the families of Paulet (or
Pawlett), Berewe (or Barrow), Lawrence
and Parker ...* Bedford: Foundry Press,
1963. Paulet and Barrow of
Gloucestershire; Lawrence of
Lancashire and Gloucestershire;
Parker of Glamorganshire and
Monmouthshire.

Peel
CHAPMAN, STANLEY D. 'The Peels in the
early English cotton industry', *Business
history* **11**, 1969, 61-89.
PEEL, JONATHAN. *The Peels: a family
sketch.* Richard Bentley and Son, 1877.
Includes folded pedigree, medieval-19th c.
Supplemented by:
Notes to 'the Peels', 1925. Lancaster: Beeley
Bros., 1925.
*Pedigree of the Right Hon. Sir Robert Peel,
Bart., and the Peels of Lancashire from
1600.* Blackburn: Thomas Briggs, 1885.

Pemberton
AXON, WILLIAM E.A. 'The Pembertons of
Aspull and Philadelphia, and some
passages in the early history of Quakers
in Lancashire', *L.C.A.S.* **30**, 1912, 153-63.
17th c.
LEIGH-PEMBERTON, JESSIE G. 'Pemberton'
Pedigree register **2**, 1910-13, 46-9. Of
Pemberton; subsequently of Torry Hill,
Kent; pedigree, 12-19th c.

Pendlebury
See Cooper

Penketh
See Ashton

Penkett
WOODS, E. CUTHBERT. 'Further notes on the Penkett family', *H.S.L.C.* 78; N.S., 42, 1926, 107-28. Includes folded pedigree, 17-19th c.

Penn
See Assheton

Percival
HEYWOOD, JAMES. 'On the family of Percival, of Allerton, Lancashire', *H.S.L.C.* 1, 1849, 61-6. Mainly 17-18th c.

Perfect
PRICE, JEAN. 'Education records at Summerseat and the family historian', *L.* 9(4), 1988, 29-32. Perfect family, late 19th c.

Peters
STEWART-BROWN, R. 'An account of the oil painting, Liverpool in 1680, with notes on the Peters family of Platbridge and Liverpool', *H.S.L.C.* 60; N.S., 24, 1908, 35-71. Peters family, 17-19th c.

Phillips
PHILLIPS, R.B. 'The Phillips family: a Lancashire branch with Yorkshire connections, 1800-1900, *L.* 8(1), 1987, 41-6.

Pickles
See Astin

Pickup
PICKUP, ALBERT. 'A Lancashire family, 6: Pickup of Darwen', *L.* 6(2), 1985, 17-20. Includes pedigree, 18-20th c.

Pilkington
HARLAND, JOHN. *Genealogy of the Pilkingtons of Lancashire (Pilkington, Rivington, Durham, Sharples, Preston, St. Helens and Sutton),* ed. W.E.A.Axon. Manchester: Charles Simms, 1875. Includes pedigrees, 14-19th c.
L., W. 'On the Pilkington pedigree', *Local notes and queries from the Manchester Guardian* 95, 1875, 1. Medieval.

PILKINGTON, JOHN. *The history of the Pilkington family of Lancashire and its branches from 1066 to 1600, compiled from ancient deeds, charters, pipe rolls, de banco rolls, final concords, wills and other authentic sources.* 3rd ed. Liverpool: C. Tinling & Co., 1912.
PILKINGTON, JOHN. 'Origin of the name Pilkington', *H.S.L.C.* 51; N.S., 15, 1899, 229-32.
PILKINGTON, JOHN. 'The early history of the Lancashire family of Pilkington, and its branches, from 1066 to 1600', *H.S.L.C.* 45; N.S., 9, 1893, 159-218. Includes folded pedigree, with list of pupils at Rivington school, 1575.
PILKINGTON, R.G. *Harland's history and pedigrees of the Pilkingtons, from the Saxon and Norman times to the present century, collected from the ancient records, deeds, charters, &c., ...* 4th ed. Dublin: Alex Thorn & Co., 1906. Includes folded pedigrees, medieval-19th c. Actually virtually a new work.
RAISON, MAUREEN. 'Pilkingtons: from Ramsbottom to New Zealand, *L.* 6(3), 1985, 34. Includes pedigree, 18-19th c.
See also Cooper and Willoughby.

Pilling
METCALFE, NORMAN. 'The memoranda of Mathias Pilling, of Bury, 1827-1913, *L.* 7(4), 1986, 30-35. Pilling family, 18-20th c.

Pinnington
PARKER, PAULINE. 'The Pinnington Saga', *L.F.H.* 4(1), 1982, 9-11. 18-19th c.

Place
TAYLOR, W.J. 'The Place family of Hoddlesden, Over Darwen, and West Bradford', *L.* 14(2), 1993, 13-19. See also 14(3), 1993, 21-6. 19-20th c.

Platt
WILLIAMS, W.OGWEN. 'The Platts of Oldham', *Caernarvonshire Historical Society transactions* 18, 1957, 75-88. 19th c.

Plungeon
See Mort

Poitou

SCHOFIELD, R. 'Roger of Poitou', *H.S.L.C.* 117, 1965, 185-90. Includes pedigrees, 11-12th c.

Pope

See Cronshaw

Postlethwaite

'The Postlethwaite family of Broughton-in-Furness', *C.F.H.S.N.* 10, 1979, 3-5. 19-20th c.

Potter

SUGDEN, A.V., & ENTWISLE, E.A. *Potters of Darwen, 1839-1939: a century of wallpaper printing by machinery.* Manchester: George Falkner & Sons, 1939. Includes folded Potter family pedigree, 17-19th c.

Prince

ROSSER, MURIEL. *The Princes of Loom Street: a cotton spinner's family, 1800-1850.* Manchester manuscripts, 2. Manchester: Historical Association, Manchester Branch, 1972. Folder containing a handbook, 6 cards, and 27 documents.

Proctor

LAVER, ANN. *Robert Proctor of Wheatley Lane, Lancashire: died 1801. Shoemaker. A history of his descendants from c.1750.* West Horsley: the author, 1989. Includes pedigrees.

Radcliffe

DARLINGTON, EVELYN M. *The Radcliffes of Leigh, Lancashire: a family memorial.* Lutterworth, privately published, 1918. 15-19th c.

HAMPSON, CHARLES P. *The book of the Radclyffes: being an account of the main descents of this illustrious family from its origin to the present day ...* Edinburgh: T. & A. Constable, 1940. Medieval-20th c., includes pedigrees. Extensive.

LEES, BARBARA M. 'The Radcliffes: a legendary link', *M.G.* 20(4), 1983, 99-102. Includes pedigree, 19-20th c.

TODD, ANDREW. 'Radcliffe, [of] Atherton, Tyldesley & Manchester', *M.G.* 19(1), 1982, 12. Pedigree, 18-19th c.

'Genealogy and biography', in HARLAND, JOHN, ed. *Collectanea relating to Manchester and its neighbourhood at various periods.* C.S., O.S., 72, 1867, 131-44. Includes notes on Radcliffe, medieval, and Strangewayes, 14-17th c.

'Memoranda relating to the family of Radcliffe, of Manchester parish, extracted from the registers of the Collegiate church', *M.G.H.* 2nd series, 4, 1892, 362-5 & 371-6. 16-18th c.

'Obits of the Radcliffes of Ordsall', *H.S.L.C.* 64; N.S., 28, 1912, 265-7. 16th c. death notices.

See also Ashawe

Radman

RUDMAN, PETER. 'Radman, Ridman, Rodman, and Rudman in North Yorkshire, West Yorkshire and Lancashire: variants of Redman', *L.* 11(2), 1990, 35-40.

Ransford

RANSFORD, ALFRED. *The origin of the Ransfords from the baronial settlement in Normandy circa 900 to the baronial settlement in England temp. Doomsday (1086), and their immediate descendants.* Mitchell, Hughes & Clarke, 1919. Of Norfolk, Lancashire, *etc.*

Ratcliffe

RATCLIFFE, JOHN G. 'Family history: Culcheth/Croft: Ratcliffe, 1678-1820', *M.G.* 22(4), 1986, 114-5. Includes pedigree.

Rathbone

MARRINER, SHEILA. *Rathbones of Liverpool, 1845-73.* Liverpool: Liverpool University Press, 1961. Includes 'abridged family tree'.

Ravald

MCALPINE, IAN. *A case study in early genealogy: the Ravalds of Manchester and Kersal 1381-1600.* Manchester: Manchester and Lancashire F.H.S., 1993.

MCALPINE, IAN. 'Venture into medieval genealogy: the Ravald family of Manchester', *M.G.* 23(3), 1987, 185-95.

MCALPINE, IAN. 'The Ravald family of Manchester and Kersal, 1483-1548', *M.G.* 23(4), 1987, 274-80.

MCALPINE, IAN. 'The Ravald family of Manchester and Kersal, 1548-1560', *M.G.* **24**(1), 1988, 20-27. Includes pedigree, 14-16th c.

MCALPINE, IAN. 'A Kersal edition', *M.G.* **29**(4), 1993, 30-33. Ravald family, 16-18th c.

Rawlinson
CUNLIFFE, LYNETTE. *The Rawlinsons of Furness, being an account and the pedigree of an old Lancashire family.* Kendal: Titus Wilson, 1978. 15-19th c., includes extracts from original sources.

Rawnson
MAUDSLEY, ANNE. 'Roger who? Or, what was your mother's maiden name?', *L.* **15**(2), 1994, 22-5. Rawnson/Rawson/Ronson/Rowlandson family, 18-19th c.

Rawson
See Rawnson and Royds

Reade
READE, ALEYN LYELL. *A family news letter from Aleyn Lyell Reade to his nephews.* [Privately printed], 1930. Reade family of Horton, Staffordshire, Liverpool, *etc.,* 18-19th c.

READE, A.L. *The Reades of Blackwood Hall in the parish of Horton, Staffordshire: a record of their descendants, with a full account of Dr. Johnson's ancestry, his kinsfolk and family connexions.* Spottiswoode & Co., 1906. Also of the Manchester district, *etc.* Includes 29 pedigrees, with many extracts from original sources.
See also Mellard

Redman
GREENWOOD, WILLIAM. *The Redmans of Levens and Harewood: a contribution to the history of the Levens family of Redman and Redmayne in many of its branches.* Kendal: Titus Wilson, 1905. Levens, Westmorland, Harewood, Yorkshire. Medieval-17th c., many pedigrees, including one of Redman of Ireby, 15-17th c.
See also Radman

Redmayne
See Redman

Remington
See Machell

Ridehalgh
See Aspinall

Ridman
See Radman

Rigby
PURSER, JOHN E. 'Rigby, Barton, Halsall & Wignall ancestors', *L.* **7**(4), 1986, 26-8. Includes pedigree, 18-19th c.

'Kenyon-Peele Hall, and the Clerks of the Peace for Lancashire', *P.N.* **4**, 1884, 143-7. Rigby and Kenyon families; includes pedigree shewing connection, 16-18th c.

Risley
'Risley of Risley, Co. Lancaster', *M.G.H.* N.S., **2**, 1877, 27-36. Pedigree, 14-18th c.
See also Culcheth

Robinson
REED, EVELYN. 'John Robinson of Burton in Kendal and Moston, coachman and census enumerator', *L.* **10**(1), 1990, 35-6. Includes pedigree, 19th c.

'Robinson family bible', *M.G.* **19**(3) 1983, 74. 18-19th c.

Rochdale
BRIERLEY, HENRY. 'The surname Rochdale', *Transactions of the Rochdale Literary & Scientific Society* **13**, 1917-19, 42-6.

Rockliff
BUSH, ADRIAN ROCKLIFFE LUBE. *A history of the Rockliff family of Liverpool.* Aughton: Cox Rockliffe, 1984. 18-20th c.

Rodman
See Radman

Rogers
See Cronshaw

Ronson
See Rawnson

Roscoe

DUNSTON, FREDERICK WARBURTON. *Roscoeana: some account of the kinsfolk of William Roscoe of Liverpool and Jane (nee Griffies) his wife.* Donhead St. Mary: privately printed, [1906]. Includes extensive pedigrees, including those of Griffies of Chester, Lace, Ambrose of Ormskirk, *etc.* 16-19th c.

Rossindall

See Lloyd

Rowlandson

See Rawnson

Royds

ROYDS, CLEMENT M., SIR. *The pedigree of the family of Royds.* Mitchell, Hughes and Clarke, 1910. 18-20th c., also of Yorkshire. Includes pedigrees of Beswicke, Calverley, Clegg, Gilbert, Hudson, Littledale, Meadowcroft, Molyneaux, Rawson, Smith and Twemlow.

'The Royds of Rochdale', *Three banks review* **19**, 1953, 44-53. 19th c.

Rudman

See Radman

Rylands

RYLANDS, J.PAUL. 'Rylands of the Rylands, within Westhoughton, Co. Lancaster', *Genealogist* **4**, 1880, 170-8.

Saint Saviour

See Statham

Samuel

HART, RONALD J. D'ARCY, ed. *The Samuel family of Liverpool and London, from 1755 onwards: a biographical and genealogical dictionary of the descendants of Emanuel Samuel.* Routledge & Kegan Paul, 1958. Includes pedigrees.

Sandiforth

PHILANDER. 'The Sandiforths', *[Manchester] City news notes and queries* **4**, 1882, 58-9. See also 66 & 69. 18th c., of Oldham.

Sandys

SANDYS, E.S. *History of the family of Sandys of Cumberland, afterwards of Furness in North Lancashire, and its branches in other parts of England and in Ireland.* 2 vols. Barrow in Furness: Barrow Printing Co., 1930. Includes pedigrees, 13-19th c. (in v.2), also index of marriages, *etc.*

VIVIAN, COMLEY. *Some notes for a history of the Sandys family of Great Britain, Ireland, and the (former) colony of Virginia, with their arms, pedigrees, portraits; illustrations of ancient seats, foundations, chantries, monuments, documents, tapestries, &c. from the twelfth century onwards,* ed. Thomas Myles Sandys. Farmer & Sons, 1907. Medieval-18th c; of Cumberland, Hampshire, Kent and Lancashire.

Sankey

BEST-GARDNER, CLEMENT SANKEY. *Memorials of the family of Sankey, A.D. 1207-1880.* Swansea: Cambrian Office, 1880. Of Lancashire, Shropshire, Bedfordshire, Buckinghamshire and Ireland.

'The Sankeys, mercers, of Ormskirk,' *Lancashire Record Office report* 1965, 37-45; 1966, 12-24. Pt. 1. 1613. Pt. 2. 1613-1636. *See also* Wild

Saxon

SAXON, JACK. 'The origin of the surname Saxon', *M.G.* **25**(2), 1989, 17-18. Medieval.

Scarisbrick

ABRAM, W.A. 'Ancient Lancashire families: the Scarisbricks of Scarisbrick', *L.C.A.N.* **2**, 1886, 211-54. 13-19th c.

CHEETHAM, F.H. 'Scarisbrick Hall, Lancashire', *L.C.A.S.* **24**, 1906, 76-104. Includes notes on the Scarisbrick family, 13-19th c.

Schofield

T., S.H.D. 'The Schofields', *Manchester notes & queries* **7**, 1888, 9-10. See also 22-3. 16-18th c.

Scholes/Scoales

FISHWICK, HENRY. 'The Scholes (or Scoales) family of Salford', *P.N.* **4**, 1884, 28-30. 17th c.

Seddon

FLETCHER, JOHN SAMUEL. *The correspondence of Nathan Walworth and Peter Seddon of Outwood, and other documents chiefly relating to the building of Ringley Chapel.* C.S., O.S., **109**, 1880. Includes folded pedigree of Seddon, 15-19th c., will of Nathan Walworth, etc.

WINTERBOTHAM, DIANA. 'Seventeenth century life in the Irwell Valley: the Seddon family of Prestolee and their neighbours', *L.C.A.S.* **84**, 1987, 64-77.

Sharples

PURCELL, MARGARET. 'A Lancashire family, 23: Sharples of Tarnacre and Goosnargh: their history from wills', *L.* **10**(3), 1989, 24-6. 17-19th c.

Shaw

CROSBY, ALAN G., ed. *The family records of Benjamin Shaw, mechanic of Dent, Dolphinholme and Preston, 1772-1841.* L.C.R.S., **130**. 1991.

SHAW, R. CUNLIFFE. 'A Lancashire clerical family of the sixteenth and seventeenth centuries', *H.S.L.C.* **115**, 1964, 41-63. Shaw family; includes pedigree, 16-17th c.

SHAW, R. CUNLIFFE. *The records of a Lancastrian family, from the XIIth to the XXth century.* Preston: Guardian Press, 1940. Shaw family; includes folded pedigrees, medieval-20th c.

See also Willoughby

Shelmerdine

OGDEN, M. 'Shelmerdine family bible', *M.G.* **19**(1) 1983, 19. 19th c.

SHELMERDINE, T. 'Extracts from church registers relating to the family of Shelmerdine', *M.G.H.* N.S., **3**, 1880, 57-8, 96-7 & 133-4. From Northenden, Lancashire, Sandbach, Cheshire, and Market Drayton, Shropshire.

Sherborn

SHERBORN, CHARLES DAVIES. *A history of the family of Sherborn.* Mitchell and Hughes, 1901. Medieval-18th c.

Sherrington

BAILEY, J.E. 'The Sherringtons of Wardley Hall, near Worsley', *L.C.A.N.* **1**, 1885, 31-8. 16th c.

Shireburne

SMITH, T.C. 'Shireburnes under persecution', *Stonyhurst magazine* **6**, 1895-8, 185-6 & 217-8. Mid 17th c.

Shuttleworth

CONROY, MICHAEL P. *Backcloth to Gawthorpe.* Nelson: Hendon Publishing, 1971. Shuttleworth family, medieval-20th c.

Simpson

COHEN, PAULINE. 'Simpson family of Ennerdale, Cumb., and the Middleton family of Corney, Bootle and Gosforth', *M.G.* **21**(1), 1985, 15-16. Pedigree, 19-20th c.

SIMPSON, STEPHEN. *Simpson: records of the ancient yeoman family of the West Riding of Yorkshire, 1544-1922.* Bemrose & Sons, 1922. Also of Preston; includes pedigree, 16-20th c., deed abstracts, *etc.*

Slone

'Information copied from an old Bible belonging to Mr. Clement Eden', *M.G.* **18**(2), 1982, 35. Slone and Hendy families, 19th c.

Smallshaw

SMALLSHAW, RONALD. 'The Smallshaws and the Bolton connection', *M.G.* **27**(4), 1991, 37-9. Medieval-17th c.

Smaltham

See Johnson

Smethurst

WOODS, ALBERT W. 'Smethurst pedigree', *M.G.H.* **2**, 1876, 214-5. 18-19th c.

Smith

DURNING-LAWRENCE., EDITH J. *Notes and illustrations concerning the family history of James Smith of Coventry (b.1731-d.1794) and his descendants.* West Norwood: Truslove & Bray, 1912. Also of Manchester and Liverpool; includes 17 'pedigree tables', 18-19th c.

See also Royds

Sourbutts

DUFFY, PEGGY. 'Sourbutts/Sowerbutts', *L.* 8(2), 1987, 42-3. Medieval-19th c.

Southworth

SOUTHWORTH, JOHN & DUDGEON, ANNE. *A history of the Southworths of Samlesbury, 1300-1890.* Boston, Lincs: J.S., 1994.

Sowerbutts

See Sourbutts

Sparling

SPARLING, JOHN. *Pages from the life of John Sparling of Petton.* Edinburgh: Riverside Press, 1904. Includes accounts of the families of Sparling of Beaumont Cote, Trafford of Trafford and Cunliffe of Cunliffe, 18th c.

Speke

MURDOCH, SOPHIA. *Record of the Speke family (Jordans, Somerset).* Reading: H.T. Morley, [1900]. Of Somerset, Devon, Yorkshire, Lancashire, Wiltshire and Berkshire.

Spencer

DAVIES, C.STELLA. *North Country bred: a working class family chronicle.* Routledge & Kegan Paul, 1963. Spencer, Booth and Davies families, 18-20th c.
See also Woodcock

Spenser

ABRAM, W.A. 'A review of the evidence on the suggested relation of the poet Spenser to the clan of Spensers in the Burnley district', *Burnley Literary and Scientific Club transactions* 4, 1886, 73-82.

FISHWICK, CAROLINE. 'Was Spenser of a Lancashire family?', *P.N.* 4, 1884, 137-40. See also 170-73, 191-200, 226-7 & 238-40. 16-17th c.

Standish

GOODRICH, MERTON TAYLOR. 'The children and grandchildren of Capt. Myles Standish', *New England historical and genealogical register* 87, 1933, 149-60. Of Lancashire and New England, *etc.,* 16-17th c.

HILL, LAWRENCE. *Gentlemen of courage, forward ... a history of the Standish family, Lancashire, from the Norman Conquest in 1066 A.D., within the context of English history to the Stuart period.* Alderley Edge: Magnolia Publishing Co., 1987. Includes pedigrees.

JOHNSON, ELEANOR. *The Standish family 1189-1920.* Wigan: Standish Local History Group, 1972. Includes folded pedigree, 17-20th c.

PORTEUS, T.C. *Captain Myles Standish: his lost lands and Lancashire connections: a new investigation.* Manchester: University Press, 1920. 16th c. descent.

PORTEUS, THOMAS CRUDDAS. 'Some recent investigations concerning the ancestry of Capt. Myles Standish', *New England historical and genealogical register* 68, 1914, 339-70. Includes calendar of 28 medieval deeds relating to the lands of the Standish family of Ormskirk; also includes pedigree, 14-16th c.

WALKER, WILLIAM. 'Duxbury in decline: the fortunes of a landed estate, 1756-1932', *H.S.L.C.* 140, 1991, 33-45. Standish family.
'A chapter of Lancashire family history: the Standishes of Duxbury and Miles Standish', *[Manchester] City news notes and queries* 5, 1883-4, 62-7. 15-18th c.

Stanley

ASPDEN, THOMAS. *Historical sketches of the House of Stanley, and biography of Edward Geoffrey, 14th Earl of Derby ...* 2nd ed. Preston: the author, 1877.

BAGLEY, J.J. *The Earls of Derby, 1485-1985.* Sidgwick and Jackson, 1985. The authoritative history of the Stanley family.

CLISSITT, WILLIE C. *Knowsley Hall.* Knowsley: Stanley Estate and Stud Company, [195-?] Stanley family.

COWARD, B. 'A crisis of the aristocracy in the sixteenth and early seventeenth centuries? The case of the Stanleys, Earls of Derby, 1506-1642', *Northern history* 18, 1982, 54-77.

COWARD, B. 'The social and political position of the Earls of Derby in later seventeenth-century Lancashire', *H.S.L.C.]* 132, 1983, 127-54.

COWARD, BARRY. *The Stanleys, Lords Stanley and Earls of Derby, 1385-1672: the origins, wealth and power of a landowning family.* C.S., 3rd series, **30**. 1983. Includes pedigree, with extensive bibliography.

DRAPER, PETER. *The History of the House of Stanley, including the sieges of Lathom House, with notices of the relative and contemporary incidents, &c.* Ormskirk: T. Hutton, 1864. 11-19th c.

FRANCE, R. SHARPE. 'On some Stanley cadets in the reign of Charles II', *H.S.L.C.* **96**, 1944, 78-80.

HOSKER, P. 'The Stanleys of Lathom and ecclesiastical patronage in the north-west of England during the fifteenth century', *Northern history* **18**, 1982, 212-29.

O., GEO. 'On the Stanley legend and the houses of Boteler, Fitz-Ailward, Latham and Stanley', *Collectanea topograpahica et genealogica* **6**, 1840, 1-21. 11-17th c.

POLLARD, WILLIAM. *The Stanleys of Knowsley: a history of that noble family, including a sketch of the political and public life of the late Right Hon. the Earl of Derby, K.G.* Frederick Warne and Co., 1869. Medieval-19th c.

RAWLINS, COSMO W.H. 'The ancestry of Lady Amelia Ann Sophia Stanley', *Genealogists' magazine* **11**, 1953, 403-9. 16-17th c.

ROSS, DAVID. *Sketch of the history of the House of Stanley and the house of Sefton.* W.S.Orr and Co., 1848. Stanley and Molyneaux families, medieval-19th c. Brief.

SEACOME, JAMES. *Memoirs, containing a genealogical and historical account of the ancient and honourable house of Stanley, from the Conquest to the death of James, late Earl of Derby, in the year 1735; as also a full description of the Isle of Man, &c.* 6th ed. Manchester: Harrop, 1783.

A history of the noble house of Stanley, from the Conquest to the present time (with considerable additions) containing a genealogical and historical account of that illustrious house ... Manchester: William Willis, 1840.

The Stanley papers. C.S., O.S., **29, 31, 66-7, & 70**. 1853-67. Pt. 1. The Earls of Derby and the verse writers of the sixteenth and seventeenth centuries, by Thomas Heywood. Pt. 2. The Derby household books, comprising an account of the household regulations and expenses of Edward and Henry, third and fourth Earls of Derby, together with a diary containing the names of the guests who visited the latter Earl at his houses in Lancashire by William Ffarington, esquire, the Comptroller, ed. F.R. Raines. Pt. 3. (3 vols.) Private devotions and miscellanies of James, Seventh Early of Derby, K.G., with a prefatory memoir and an appendix of documents, ed. F. R. Raines.

For other works on the Stanley family, see *Cheshire: a genealogical bibliography, vol.2.*

Stansfeld

STANSFELD, JOHN. *History of the family of Stansfeld of Stansfield in the parish of Halifax and its numerous branches.* Leeds: Goodall and Suddick, 1885. Also of Burnley. Extensive; includes pedigrees, medieval-19th c. and many extracts from original sources.

Stapleton

GIBLIN, J.F. 'The Stapleton-Bretherton family and the mission of St. Bartholomew's, Rainhill', *N.W.C.H.* **9**, 1982, 10-17. Primarily concerned with the mission, rather than the family. Many names, 18-20th c.

Starkie

RYLANDS, JOHN PAUL. *The Starkie family of Pennington and Bedford, in the parish of Leigh, Co. Lancaster.* Leigh: [Leigh Chronicle], 1880. 16-17th c.

Statham

STATHAM, S.P.H. *The descent of the family of Statham, containing an account of the Saint-Saviours, Viscounts of the Cotentin, the barony of Malpas, Co. Chester, the Lymmes of Lymme, Co. Chester, the Bolds of Bold, Co. Lancaster, the Stathums of Stathum, Co. Chester, the Stathams of Morley, Co. Derby, and of Leicestershire, Australia and U.S.America.* Times Book Co., [1925]. Includes folded pedigrees, medieval-20th c.

STEWART-BROWN, R. 'Pedigree of Statham (Liverpool and New Zealand branch) from 1716', *H.S.L.C.* **80**, 1928, 203-20.

Stephenson
STEPHENSON, ALLEN. 'Stephenson of Pennington (Furness) and Heysham', *L.* 6(4), 1985, 29-35. Includes line pedigree, 17-20th c.

Stinchcombe
See Davies

Stockdale
CHALONER, W.H. 'The Stockdale family, the Wilkinson brothers and the cotton mills at Cark-in-Cartmel, 1782-1800', *C.W.A.A.S.Tr.* N.S., **64**, 1964, 356-72.

Stones
C. 'Family of Stones', *M.G.H.* N.S., **1**, 1874, 48. Parish register extracts from Cartmel.

Stopford
NICHOLSON, FRANCIS, & AXON, ERNEST. 'Rev. Joshua Stopford and the Stopfords of Audenshaw', *L.C.A.S.* **33**, 1915, 205-15. 17-18th c.

Storey
[RIGBYE, R.] *Storeys of old: historical, biographical and genealogical observations on the Storey and Story family: prominent members of the same of the four northern counties - Northumberland, Cumberland, Durham and Westmorland, including the branches settled in Lancaster and Furness.* Preston: Exors of C. W. Whitehead, 1920. Extensive; includes pedigrees, medieval-20th c., and numerous extracts from original sources.

Strangwayes
STRANGWAYES, THOMAS EDWARD. *Materials for a genealogical history of the house of Strangwayes, sometime of Strangwayes Hall, in the County of Lancaster.* 2 vols. Privately printed, 1894-5. 14-19th c., also of Shapwick, Somerset.
See also Radcliffe.

Street
BARLOW, ANGELA & SMITH, BETTE JANE. 'The key of the Streets', *M.G.* 19(1), 1983, 23-5. Includes pedigree of Street of Alt, 18-20th c.

Strettle
See Hulme

Streynsham
See Master

Strutt
FITTON, R.S. *The Strutts and the Arkwrights, 1758-1830: a study of the early factory system.* Manchester: Manchester University Press, 1958.

Sunderland
HITCH, ALAN. 'A Lancashire family, 10: Sunderland of Withins, Lidgate & Rawtenstall', *L.* 7(2), 1986, 22-4. Pedigree, 17-20th c.

Sutcliffe
TRAVIS, JOHN. 'A Lancashire family, 8: Sutcliffe of Todmorden', *L.* 6(4), 1985, 17-20. Includes pedigree, 18-20th c.
'Sutcliffe family bible', *M.G.* 15(2), 1979, 40. 18-19th c.

Sutton
'Some research into the Suttons', *M.G.* Autumn 1973, 4-6. 18-20th c.
See also Mort

Swainson
C., H.S. 'Swainson: Cowper: Cowper-Essex', *Pedigree register* **1**, 1907-10, 28-30. Of Hawkshead; pedigree, 18-19th c.
HEALY, HOPE FRANCIS. *An historical narrative of a Swainson family from the West Yorkshire and Lancashire counties of England.* Decorah, Iowa: Anundsen Publishing, 1993. Includes pedigree, 16-20th c.

Swarbreck
See also Harrison

Talbot
BARTLETT, J.G. *The English ancestry of Peter Talbot of Dorchester, Mass.* Boston, Massachusetts: Privately printed, 1917. Of Carr Hall, Blackburn. Medieval-17th c.

Tatham
CHIPPINDALL, W.H. 'Hipping Hall', *C.W.A.A.S.Tr.* N.S., **32**, 1932, 68-74. Includes pedigree of Tatham, 17-20th c.

CHIPPINDALL, W.H. 'The Tatham families of Burrow, Tunstall, Cantsfield, and Lowfields', *C.W.A.A.S.Tr.* N.S., **33**, 1933, 98-112. Includes folded pedigrees, 17-20th c.

Tatlock

PATCHETT, ALFRED. *Memorials (1547 to 1757) of the Tatlocks of Cunscough within Melling, near Liverpool.* Liverpool: Privately printed, 1901.

Tatton

HALL, BETTE W. 'Tatton family pedigree chart', *M.G.* **18**(4) 1982, 98-101. 14-20th c.

Taylor

COHEN, BARBARA. A. 'Family history', *Eccles and District History Society lectures* 1985-87, 54-76. Taylor family, 19-20th c.

TAYLOR, W.J. 'They all came from Manchester', *L.* **12**(4), 1991, 20-29. Taylor family, 19-20th c.

WEST, JOHN L. *The Taylors of Lancashire: bonesetters and doctors, 1750-1890.* Worsley: H. Duffy. 1977.

'A Lancashire family: Taylor of Rossendale', *L.* **5**(1), 1984, 18-25. Includes pedigree, 19-20th c.

Tetlow

See Wild

Thompson

THOMPSON, NORAH B. *Notes on A.Atwood Thompson and on some of his ancestors and descendants, and on related families Eltonhead and Thompson.* Privately printed, 1966. Includes pedigrees, 14-19th c., also of the United States.

'Francis Thompson, the poet', *Pedigree register* **2**, 1910-13, 353-7. Includes pedigree of Thompson, of Rutland, Lancashire, *etc.,* 19-20th c.

Thorniley

See Brooke

Thursby

CHAPPLES, LESLIE. *From Ormerod to Thursby.* Twangings Press, 1979. Thursby family, 19-20th c. Includes folded pedigree.

L[ITTLEDALE], W.A. *Some notes on the families of Thursby, of Abington, Co. Northants., Hargreaves of Ormerod House, Co. Lancaster, and Thursby, of Ormerod House.* Brighton: H. and C. Treacher, 1908. Includes pedigree, 17-19th c.

Tobin

LYNN, MARTIN. 'Trade and politics in 19th century Liverpool: the Tobin and Horsfall families and Liverpool's African trade', *H.S.L.C.* **142**, 1993, 99-120.

Tonge

FISHWICK, HENRY. 'Tonge Hall, in the parish of Prestwich-cum-Oldham', *L.C.A.S.* **10**, 1892, 25-32. Brief note on Tonge family, 14-18th c.

TONGE, WILLIAM ASHETON. 'Tonge family of Tonge Hall, par. Prestwich, Co. Lancaster', *Genealogical magazine* **3**, 1899-1900, 349-52 & 406-10; **4**, 1900-1901, 46-50. Includes extracts from parish registers and wills, with pedigree, 17-18th c., *etc.*

Topham

TOPHAM, B.H. 'An account of the Topham family', *M.G.* **21**(3), 1985, 81-5. 18-19th c.

Touchet

HIGMAN, JULIAN. 'A Lancashire family, 17: Touchet of Warrington, Manchester and London', *L.* **9**(1), 20-33. See also **9**(4), 1988, 14-17. Includes pedigree, 17-18th c.

Towneley

ABRAM, W.A. 'Ancient Lancashire families, II: the Towneleys of Dutton', *L.C.A.N.* **2**, 1885, 182-90. 15-18th c.

ALGER, J.G. 'The Towneleys in Paris, 1709-80: the translator of *Hudibras*' *P.N.* **3**, 1883, 84-6 & 144-6. See also 241-6, & **4**, 1884, 119.

CHAPPLES, L. *Noblesse oblige: a Towneley chronicle of historical fact, marriage links, and notable family associations.* Podiham: Burnley and District Historical Society, 1987. Towneley family, medieval-20th c.

CHAPPLES, LESLIE. *The Towneleys of Towneley: a chronicle of the life and times of the later Towneleys.* Burnley: the author, 1976. Medieval-20th c.

KANDEL, EDWARD M. 'Two Townleys', *Coat of arms* N.S., 3(110), 1979, 158-60. Includes pedigree of Townley, 16-17th c.

YATES, GEO. C. 'The Towneleys of Towneley', *L.C.A.S.* 10, 1892, 86-91. Medieval-17th c.

'Marriages of the Towneleys', *P.N.* 4, 1884, 94-5. 17-18th c.

'The Towneley library, *P.N.* 3, 1883, 187-92. Includes pedigree, 17-19th c.

Townsend

DEMPSEY, MARGARET J. 'Family migrations & the censuses (illustrated by the Townsend and Fairclough families of Preston)', *L.* 13(3), 1992, 26-9. Includes simplified pedigree, 19th c.

Trafford

BIRD, W.H.B. 'The Trafford legend', *Ancestor* 9, 1904, 65-82; 10, 1904, 73-82. See also 12, 1904, 42-55.

BURNE, HENRY F., SIR. *Pedigree and quarterings of De Trafford, compiled from the records of the Heralds College, Record Office, probate registries and other reliable sources.* Privately printed, 1890. 11-19th c.

RICHARDS, W.S.G. *The history of the De Traffords of Trafford, circa A.D. 1000-1893, including the royal and baronial descents of the family.* Plymouth: W.H. Luke, [1893?] Includes numerous pedigrees.

See also Sparling

Travers

'Travers family', *M.G.H.* N.S., 4, 1884, 93-4. Of Liverpool; 18th c. written notes from a printed book.

Travis

TRAVIS, JOHN. *Genealogical memorials of the Travis family of Blackley, Manchester, Inchfield, Walsden, Todmorden, and Heyside, High Crompton, Oldham, &c., &c., and connections with other local families.* Walsden: Fletcher, 1893. 16-19th c.

Tunstall

CHIPPINDALL, W.H. 'Tunstall of Thurland Castle', *C.W.A.A.S.Tr.* N.S., 28, 1928, 292-313. Includes pedigree, 13-16th c.

Turnough

BOULTON, KEN, & BOULTON, MARY. 'The family of Turnough of Binns, in Butterworth', *L.* 7(3), 1986, 34-7. 17th c.

Turton

TURTON, W.H. *The early Lancashire Turtons up to A.D.1400.* Frome: Butler & Tanner, 1937. Includes medieval pedigree.

TURTON, W.H. 'The early Lancashire Turtons up to A.D.1400', *Genealogists' magazine,* 6, 1932-4, 529-46. See also 564-5.

Tweedale

TISDALL, M.S. 'Note by Mr. John Tweedale of Healey, near Whitworth', *L.* 2(9), 1979, 16-17. 19th c. entries from the Tweedale family bible.

Twemlow

See Royds

Tyldesley

LUNN, JOHN. *The Tyldesleys of Lancashire: the rise and fall of a great patrician family.* Altrincham: St. Anns Press, 1906. Medieval-18th c.

Tyson

RAMSDALE, C.N. 'Tysons of Wasdalehead, Maryport and Liverpool', *C.F.H.S.N.* 60, 1991, 18-20. Includes pedigree, 18-19th c.

Urm(e)stone

O., GEO. 'A genealogical certificate, compiled temp Henry VI, as to the descent of the Lordship of Urmestone, Co. Lancaster from the grantee of Adam de Urmestone to the Hides', *Collectanea topographica et genealogica* 8, 1843, 146-52. Includes medieval pedigrees of Urmestone and Hide.

PINK, W.D. 'Urmiston of Westleigh and Bradshaw of Fennington, Co. Lancaster', *Genealogist* N.S., **17**, 1901, 14-16. Pedigrees 13-17th c.

Urswick
URWICK, THOMAS A. *Records of the family of Urswyck, Urswick, or Urwick,* ed. Wm. Urwick. Gibbs & Bamforth, 1893. Includes pedigree, 17-19th c. Also of Yorkshire and various other counties.

Urwick
See Urswick

Waddington
WADDINGTON, JOHN. *Who's who in the family of Waddington.* Wada, 1934. Medieval-20th c. Brief biographies of numerous family members.

Walcot
WALCOT, MICHAEL. 'An Ormskirk confectioner', *L.F.H.S.J.* 3(1), 1981, 6-9. Includes pedigee of Walcot, 18-19th c.

Walker
BAGGS, DAVID WALKER. 'The problems of tracing a family with a common name in 19th century Lancaster County, England', *M.G.* 26(3), 1990, 27-8. Walker and Cook families, 19th c.
WALKER, ARTHUR, NOEL. *The Walker family, 1681 to 1946: the story of William Walker and his family's associations with Bolton.* Bolton: Tillotsons, 1947.

Waller
See Dent

Wallwork
MEALING, KATHY. Wallwork of Bolton', *L.* 6(4), 1985, 24-5. Includes pedigree, 19-20th c.

Walmesley
BRIGG, MARY. 'The Walmesleys of Dunkenhalgh: a family of Blackburn Hundred in the Elizabethan and Stuart periods', *L.C.A.S.* **75-6**, 1965-6, 72-102.

Walton
MARGERISON, H. *A brief history of the Waltons of Marsden Hall (Nelson) and of Altham.* Nelson: Caffry & Priestley, 1926.
See also Deacon

Walworth
See Seddon

Warburton
'A Bolton wanderer, or, how much of family legend is truth or fiction?', *M.G.* 21(1), 1985, 37-5 & 40. Warburton family; includes pedigree, 19-20th c.

Waring
DEMPSEY, MARGARET. 'A Lancashire family 12: Waring of North Meols & Ulnes Walton', *L.* 7(4), 1986, 23-6. Includes pedigree, 18-20th c.

Washington
PAPE, THOMAS. *Warton and George Washington's ancestors.* Morecambe: Visitor Printing Works, 1913. 16-18th c.
PEARSON, ALEXANDER. 'The Westmorland and Lancashire Washingtons', in *The doings of a country solicitor.* Kendal: Titus Wilson & Son, 1947, 152-67.
PAPE, THOMAS. *The Washingtons and the manor of Warton.* Morecombe: The Visitor, 1948. Includes various pedigrees, 16-17th c.
WHITMAN, HENRY. 'The Washingtons and their connection with Warton', in *The Castle Howell school record ...* Lancaster: R.& G. Brash, 1888, 192-204. Includes folded pedigree, medieval-18th c.

Watkinson
See Cronshaw

Watmough
WHATMORE, GEOFFREY. 'The Watmoughs of Prescot', *L.F.H.S.J.* 2(2), 1978, 76-7. 16-17th c.

Watson
WATSON, REX. 'Henry Watson: a favourite ancestor', *L.* 5(1), 1984, 8-13. See also **10**(3), 1989, 30-35. Of Burnley, 19th c.

Werden
See Worden

Whalley
'The Whalley family of Lancaster', *L.C.A.N.* **1**, 1885, 159-60. 18th c., from a family bible.
See also Master

Whatmough

'Whatmough of Rochdale, Bacup & Manchester', *L.* 5(2), 1894, 18-19. Pedigree, 17-20th c.

Whitaker

COLLINSON, H. 'An account of the family of Whitaker of Warwickshire and Lancashire, with their Cheshire connections', *North Cheshire family historian* 6(4), 1979, 101-5; 7(1), 1980, 5-9. Medieval-19th c.

White

GARSIDE, LUKE. 'The White family', *[Manchester] City news notes and queries* 8, 1889-90, 117-8. See also *passim.* 18-19th c.

MORLING, LORELEY A. 'The White family: Leitrim to Lidcombe *via* Lancashire', *L.* 13(2), 1992, 16-25. Includes pedigrees of White and Robinson, 19th c.

'The family of Dr. White of Manchester', *P.N.* 2, 1882, 274. Extracts from family bible, 18th c.

Whiteside

COOKSON, MICHAEL. 'Illegitimacy at Marton and Lytham: Whiteside, Parkinson and Knight', *L.* 12(1), 1991, 43-6. 19-20th c.

Whitestones

'The Whitestones family of Ormskirk: bearwards in the early seventeenth century', *Lancashire Record Office report* 1978, 45-8.

Whittingham

'A pedigree of the Cheshire families of Whittingham and Berington, drawn on vellum and painted by the third Randle Holmes of Chester in 1664', *Genealogist* N.S., 30, 1914, 145-9. Of Cheshire and Lancashire.

Wightman

See Master

Wignall

See Rigby

Wild

'Family register taken from a family bible: Wild, Hollingworth, Sankey, Longmoor, Tetlow', *M.G.* N.S., 2, 1965, 5-6. 19-20th c.

Wilkinson

See Cowlishaw and Stockdale

Willard

See Dunster

Williamson

ABEL, ROBERT. 'Family bible entries', *L.* 12(3), 1991, 40-41. Williamson family, 1864-1924.

Willoughby

HIGSON, P.J. 'The barony of Willoughby of Parham', *Genealogists' magazine* 15(1), 1965-8, 1-14. Descent to Leigh, Dawes, Fisher and Shaw, *etc.*, 16-20th c.

HIGSON, P.J.W. 'A dissenting northern family: the Lancashire branch of the Willoughbys of Parham', *Northern history* 7, 1972, 31-53.

WILLOUGHBY-HIGSON, PHILLIP. *The bizarre barons of Rivington.* Newcastle: North Briton Press, 1965. Willoughby family, 17-18th c.

'Rivington and the Willoughby and Pilkington families', in BARTON, B.T., ed. *Historical gleanings of Bolton and District [second series].* Bolton: Daily Chronicle Office, 1882, 214-316. 16-18th c.

Wilson

FOSTER, JOSEPH. *The pedigree of Wilson of High Wray and Kendal, and the families connected with them.* Head, Hole & Co., 1871. 17-19th c., includes list of 'matches'. *See also* Carus

Winder

WINDER, THOMAS H. *Records and reminiscences of some of the Winder family for 200 years.* Bolton: W. S. Barlow and Co., 1902. Includes folded pedigree, 17-20th c.

Winkley

WINKLEY, WILLIAM. *Documents relating to the Winkley family.* [ ]: Harrow Press, 1863. Of Lancashire, Lincolnshire, Middlesex, *etc.*, includes wills, extracts from parish registers and records *etc.*, with pedigrees, medieval-18th c.

Winstanley

See Cropper

Wither

BIGG-WITHER, REGINALD F. *Materials for a history of the Wither family.* Winchester: Warren & Son, 1907. 12-19th c., of Lancashire, Hampshire, *etc.* Includes wills, parish register extracts, pedigrees, *etc.*

Wolsey

See Cropper

Wood

COUPE, GLADYS, & LEWIS, ORRELL F. *The Wood family of Lancashire, England, & Gloucester County, New Jersey.* New Jersey: Gloucester County Historical Society, 1985. Of Tottington.

Woodcock

GRAY, ANDREW E.P. *Woodcock of Cuerden, of Newburgh, and of Wigan, Co. Lancaster.* Canterbury: Ginder, 1882. 16-19th c., includes pedigrees of Spencer, Baldwin, Holme, Hastings, Bankes and Leigh.

Woodhead

FRENCH, JENNY. 'A Lancashire family, 26: Woodhead of Newbiggin (Northumberland) and Shawforth Valley', *L.* 11(2), 1990, 25-9. Includes pedigree, 18-20th c.

Woods

G., J.D. 'The Wood family', in BARTON, B.T., ed. *Historical gleanings of Bolton and District [second series]* Bolton: Daily Chronicle Office, 1882, 45-7. 18-19th c., of Bolton.

Woolfall

WOOLFALL, RICHARD J. 'Woolfall', *L.F.H.S.J.* 2(5), 1980, 95-103. Medieval-18th c.

Worden

WORDEN, ERIC. 'Worden/Werden of Clayton-le-Woods, Preston and New England', *L.* 11(1), 1990, 27-9. Includes pedigree, 16-17th c.

Wrigley

'Wrigley family of Liverpool', *M.G.* 16(4), 1980, 108. Pedigree, 19-20th c.

Yannes

HIGSON, C.E. 'The Yannes family of Lees', *L.C.A.S.* 47, 1930-31, 172-7.

Yarker

YARKER, JOHN. *Genealogy of the surname Yarker, with the Leyburn and several allied families resident in the counties of Yorkshire, Durham, Westmorland and Lancashire, including all of the name in Cumberland, Canada, America and Middlesex.* Manchester: A.M.Petty & Co., 1882. Includes extensive pedigrees, medieval-19th c.

Yates

RUNYON, ETHEL DALE. 'David Yates family: Lancashire, Cheshire, and points beyond', *M.G.* 30(3), 1994, 10-14. 18-19th c.

Family Name Index

IMPORTANT

This is an index to sections 1 to 6 only; it does **not** include the many family names listed in section 7. Since they are in alphabetical order, it would be superfluous to index them.

Place Name Index

58

59

Author Name Index

64